Historic Houses

TIME-LIFE BOOKS

Alexandria, Virginia

A Country House Tour

TIME-LIFE BOOKS

Alexandria, Virginia

A Country House Tour

*beautiful homes that
capture the flavor
of the past*

A REBUS BOOK

C O N T E N T S

INTRODUCTION

6

The Farmhouse Tradition

Historic Homestead · Sponging a Wall · Sponging Variations
A Victorian Retreat · Quilts of the 1930s · An Ohio Landmark
White Ironstone · Farmhouse Living
American Almanacs

8

Country Conversions

Schoolhouse Revival · The Country Schoolhouse
New Life for an Old Barn · American Barns
A Tavern Reborn · Tavern Drinks

60

Cabin Living

A Texas Past · Miniature Log Cabins
Log Cabin Pleasures · Appalachian Baskets

88

Country in the City

A Country Town House
Decorative Dutch Wall Tiles · An Eclectic Apartment
Making a Ruffled Pillow

110

Preserving the Past

Attention to Detail · Traditional Swag Curtain
Asymmetric Swag Curtain · A New Classic
Hand-Carved Bird Trees · A Country Cape
Decor for the Door

130

SELECTED READING

168

CREDITS

170

INDEX

172

ACKNOWLEDGMENTS

175

T his volume invites you to visit fourteen remarkable houses, all testaments to the time and energy their owners have devoted to them. The buildings range in type from a 1769 stone farmstead in Lancaster County, Pennsylvania, to a newly built Cape Cod cottage designed by its owners to replicate the classic early Cape they never managed to buy. There are rustic log cabins refurbished for contemporary living, and city apartments that have gained a country look through a careful choice of furniture and accessories. And then there are the homes that were never intended to be homes at all: a one-room schoolhouse, an 18th-century tavern, and a 19th-century horse barn, which, with imagination and good planning, have all been converted into comfortable residences that capture a flavor of the past.

While they may seem an eclectic choice, the houses in this volume actually have quite a lot in common—as do their owners. Many of the old structures were in disuse or disrepair when they were purchased, and few looked anything like they look today, outside or in. It took people with vision to recognize the potential of these buildings to become distinctive residences. Vision—and perhaps naiveté. As the owner of one early farmhouse put it, "If I had known what I was getting into, I'm not sure I would have gotten into it."

Indeed, it seems that few of the individuals who worked on old buildings realized just how many hundreds of hours it can take to restore a house to its original appearance or to remodel it to accommodate a modern lifestyle. And yet those hours—often turning into years—were invested in these projects, sometimes with the labor being done by the owners themselves.

Stucco was removed from brick or stone exteriors, linoleum was peeled off hardwood floors, plasterboard was stripped away to reveal original beaded-board paneling. In most cases, historical accuracy was an important issue, but at the same time few of the homeowners were willing to sacrifice comfort; where necessary, wings were built, ceilings raised, and essential modern fixtures installed, particularly in kitchens and baths. Where rooms were dark, skylights might be added to let in more light. Where rooms were small, walls were knocked down to open up the spaces and make them more useful. Where no storage space existed, closets and cabinets were often constructed.

A similar approach was taken in furnishing these homes to be comfortable and welcoming. Many of the houses contain exceptionally fine collections of antiques, but none of them has a museumlike or impersonal decor. In touring each, you will quickly see that while they embrace the past, they are clearly the homes of people who enjoy living in the present.

The Farmhouse Tradition

preserving the homes
of rural America

Perhaps because the family farm is steadily disappearing from the American landscape, the idea of owning an old farmhouse is particularly appealing to those who are interested in preserving the past or in getting back to the land. As this chapter reveals, the farmhouse tradition in America encompasses a wide range of periods and styles as well as regional and ethnic influences. Although the houses that farmers erected for themselves were usually small to allow for efficient heating, additions were often built as finances permitted. Over time, succeeding generations would make further "improvements," and the lines and detailing of the original farmhouse might disappear altogether.

Through hard work and perseverance, the families who live in the old farmhouses shown on the following pages have managed to bring their homes back to their early appearances. The great amount of research and care that went into these preservation efforts is evident in each; equally apparent are the satisfaction and rewards those efforts have yielded.

Simple paneling preserves the country look of an 1890s farmhouse entry hall.

Historic Homestead

Distinguished by a steeply pitched metal roof, the late-18th-century barn above, part of the old Stauffer farmstead, may have been built at the same time as the house.

The owner of this restored Pennsylvania residence and accompanying barn had been looking for an old stone farmhouse for several years before finding the 18th-century homestead, located in Lancaster County. And even after finally finding it, he was not sure he wanted it: the masonry walls were obscured by stucco, one fireplace was bricked over, a second had been removed, and the whole house was in a general state of disrepair.

Yet, while many of the building's early features were unrecognizable, the raised plaster inscription "CST 1769" in the entrance hall indicated that, at the very least, the house was an old one. As the debris left by previous owners was cleaned up and the many "modernizations" removed, it also became increasingly apparent to the owner that he had something important

Continued

Restoration of the Pennsylvania-German farmhouse at right involved both the 1769 stone portion and the mid-19th-century frame addition.

on his hands. Wanting to proceed cautiously, he called in preservation experts to help him identify which features were significant and decide how they should be restored. "The experts located original architectural elements, obscured over the years, that showed the structure was historically important," he says. "Knowing that, I felt an obligation to preserve the house's past."

That past, as it turned out, was an interesting one. Records revealed that the original owner was a Mennonite farmer named Christian Stauffer, one of the many German immigrants to settle in Pennsylvania in the 18th century. Stauffer arrived in Philadelphia in 1749 and later moved to Lancaster County, building the stone farmhouse on a three-hundred-acre tract in 1769. Unlike his neighbors, most of whom lived in log cabins or roughly laid fieldstone dwellings, Stauffer—

Continued

The dining room, left, was originally a kitchen, and features a walk-in cooking fireplace. The stenciled flower motif and red wash on the walls in this room and in the stairwell, above, are based on traces of 18th-century decoration discovered in the house.

The bench above is a copy of an original built-in; such seating was common in European homes and was often reproduced in America by German immigrants. The stenciled motifs were adapted from traditional German designs.

who was evidently quite prosperous—erected a fine, nine-room residence of hand-dressed limestone. The house, now listed on the National Register of Historic Places, is not only one of the few extant local examples of 18th-century Pennsylvania-German architecture, but it is also the earliest documented Germanic farmhouse in the area to incorporate elements of the English Georgian style, including a center hallway.

Given the significance of the homestead, it seemed only logical to take it back to its early appearance. The stucco was removed from the original stone section; the front door hood and

Continued

Following a German custom, the parlor, left, contains a so-called "holy corner," where family members would have gathered to read the Bible traditionally kept there. The raised plaster catherine wheel on the ceiling is one of only two known examples in existence.

Painted with designs common to Lancaster County, the doors were designed to complement the colorful wall finishes in the house. The subtle striations on the kitchen door, above, were inspired by the markings in the stone next to it. The door at right was washed in a honey shade to harmonize with the yellow paint in the parlor.

Turquoise, the color on the bedroom door above, was one of the original hues used in the house. The bird on the red door panel at left is a traditional Pennsylvania-German motif; the design on the blue panel was created by pressing corncobs and wax paper into wet paint.

The kitchen, right, is housed in the 19th-century frame addition. The simple beaded-board cabinetry, teak countertop, and stenciled floor pattern harmonize with the look of the earlier stone section of the house.

the two entryway benches were reconstructed.

Although the wood-frame wing that had been added to one end of the stone building in the 1800s was not built by Christian Stauffer, it was retained, and is used to house the kitchen, laundry, and bathrooms. To blend in with the earlier structure, the refurbished exterior of the wing now displays a shed-roofed porch, a typical feature of early Pennsylvania-German dwellings.

Many original elements on the interior of the house have been restored, including the distinctive six-pointed plaster rosette, known as a catherine wheel, on the parlor ceiling. Although the motif had been shaved down to the ceiling plane, its outline remained and it was possible for a craftsman to re-create it.   *Continued*

Among the furnishings in the dining area of the kitchen, above, are a 19th-century Pennsylvania hutch-table and corner cupboard.

The bedroom above features a 19th-century painted rope bed and an Amish quilt made around 1860.

The interior is also notable for its remarkable painted decoration, based on the traces of early finishes and stenciled motifs that were uncovered during the renovation. As in days past, the rooms are washed in rich hues of turquoise, yellow, and rose. Whenever possible, the colors and designs were replicated, but where the stencil patterns were too indistinct to copy, traditional Pennsylvania-German patterns were used to approximate the old designs. The striking paint treatments are complemented by the decorative finishes on the doors, which were all reproduced from an 18th-century paneled original that was found in the barn.

A careful selection of 18th-century pieces— as well as high-quality reproductions—contributes to the overall effect. Among the antique furnishings are many from Pennsylvania, including a tall-case clock, a trestle table, and a carved plank chair. Nearly indistinguishable from antiques are two sets of ladder-back chairs and a pencil-post bed made by contemporary local craftsmen known for their traditional workmanship. In order to capture a sense of how the house might have looked in Stauffer's time, the arrangements are simple. There are no rugs, and few accessories; the rich colors and spirit of the past speak for themselves.

An 1844 Pennsylvania woven coverlet brings color to the master bedroom, above; the pencil-post bed is a reproduction.

SPONGING A WALL

Of the many distinctive wall treatments that can be accomplished with paint, sponging is among the easiest to do. In this technique, a dampened sponge is used to dab one or two paint colors in a random pattern over a solid base color. (The directions opposite are for sponging two colors over a base.)

The possibilities are almost limitless: pale colors can be used over a dark base, or darker tones over a pale base, and the sponging can be dense or light. Depending on the colors used and the method of application, the result could be a subtle look or one that is dramatically mottled, as above. For a sampling of different color combinations and the effects they can produce, turn to the chart on pages 24 and 25; be sure, however, to experiment with your own ideas as well.

Use fast-drying latex paint and work with a natural sea sponge (preferably one filled with good-size holes) that fits easily in the hand. Before you start sponging a wall, practice your dabbing technique on a sheet of paper. Dab quickly, shifting the position of your hand and turning the sponge as you do so; keep your touch light to avoid smudging the paint. As soon as you feel comfortable with the technique you will be ready to begin.

A. The first sponging color is applied with a light touch; plenty of the base color shows through.

B. The second color is sponged on sparingly, to overlap the base color and the first sponged color, for a cohesive look.

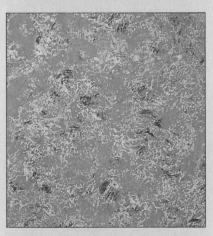

C. Together, the three colors create a marble-like finish. If desired, additional paint can be dabbed on for touchups.

MATERIALS

For a wall area measuring approximately 350 square feet, you will need one half gallon each of primer and base-coat paint. For sponging colors, allow one quart for each color that you will be using. Eggshell- or flat-finish paint is suggested for both the base coat and the sponged colors.

· Latex interior primer ·
· Latex paint for base coat · 2 shades of latex paint for sponging ·
· Paint roller and roller tray · 2 shallow pans ·
· 2 medium-size sea sponges · Scrap paper for testing sponge prints ·
· Plastic sheeting or painting tarpaulin ·
· Masking tape ·

DIRECTIONS

1. Spread the plastic sheeting or tarpaulin on the floor. Using the masking tape, cover any parts of the window and door frames, moldings, fixtures, and baseboards that are adjacent to the painting area. (Be sure to remove the tape soon after the paint has dried.)

2. Keeping the work area well ventilated, prepare the walls with one coat of primer according to the manufacturer's directions, and let dry.

3. Using the paint roller, cover the walls with the base color and allow the paint to dry thoroughly. Repeat with a second coat.

4. Pour the first sponging color into a pan. Dampen a sea sponge with water and squeeze it almost dry. Dip the sponge in the paint and dab off excess paint on the scrap paper until the prints have a delicate appearance. (Wet-looking sponge prints indicate too much paint.)

5. Once you have the desired amount of paint on the sponge, dab the sponge on the wall in an even rhythm and using a light quick touch. Keep the sponge prints spaced apart to allow the base color to show through (Illustration A). Additional paint can always be sponged on later. Repeat, blotting excess paint off on the scrap paper after each dip, until the walls are covered. Allow the paint to dry thoroughly.

6. Pour the second sponging color into a pan. Using a clean sea sponge, apply the color to accent some of the background areas, overlapping the first sponged prints to create a cohesive, dappled look (Illustration B). Allow the paint to dry thoroughly. Touch up with additional paint if necessary.

TIPS

◆ Be sure each coat of paint is completely dry before applying the next.

◆ Vary the position of both your hand and the sponge to avoid one-direction sponging patterns.

◆ Keep the sponge pliable and fluffy while you work by rinsing it in water periodically; be sure to squeeze out any excess water each time.

◆ For hard-to-reach corners, use a small piece of sponge. Blend the paint carefully with the overall pattern.

◆ If the total effect is too strong or too pale, you can sponge on some of the base color to correct it.

Sponging Variations

MONOCHROMATIC COLOR SCHEMES

◆ Monochromatic color schemes, in which shades of the same color are used, work well because the colors harmonize naturally. For each of the samples at right, the base color was simply mixed with white to make the sponging color. When only a small amount of white is added, the sponged effect will be subtle; adding more white creates a paler shade that provides a stronger contrast with the base color. The density of the sponge prints also affects the overall look: the more closely the prints are spaced, the more the sponging color dominates.

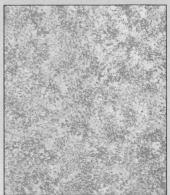

Above left, pale rose is sponged sparingly on a rose base; above right, the same pale rose is sponged more densely.

TWO-COLOR COMBINATIONS

◆ Two-color sponging combinations, shown on the samples at right, are created by applying a single color over a base color from a different color family. From a distance, a two-color combination gives the overall effect of a third color: a pink wall sponged with soft yellow, for instance, appears as peach. Avoid combining complementary colors, such as orange and blue, which are opposites on the color wheel; they will appear as muddy gray. For the most subtle effect, work with colors that are closely related in value (the degree of light and dark in a color). The more dissimilar the values, the more dramatic the contrast will be.

Blue, sponged lightly, above left, and densely, above right, has a lighter value than the dark green base, providing a strong contrast.

THREE-COLOR COMBINATIONS

◆ In three-color sponging, two colors are applied over a base color to produce a richly textured look. Three soft, related hues work well together for a subtle effect; for accent, the second sponging color can be a darker or brighter hue. When using three colors, it is especially important to do a color test on paper—varying the density of the sponge prints—before working directly on the wall.

Above left, blue-gray is sponged lightly, and beige densely, on a blue base; above right, the blue-gray is sponged more densely.

Above left, pale green is sponged on a medium-green base; above right, an even paler green is sponged more densely.

Above left, medium plum is sponged on a dark plum base; above right, pale plum is sponged in the same density.

Red sponged lightly on a maroon base, above left, appears brown. With denser sponging, above right, the overall effect is dark red.

Pink is sponged lightly on a beige base, above left. With denser sponging, above right, the overall effect is pink.

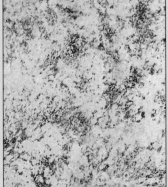

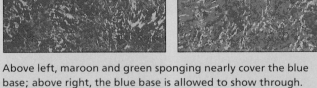

Above left, maroon and green sponging nearly cover the blue base; above right, the blue base is allowed to show through.

Above left, equal amounts of red and yellow are sponged on an orange base; above right, the yellow is sponged more densely.

A Victorian Retreat

O f all the romantic house styles that were fashionable during the Victorian era, none, perhaps, was more popular than the Queen Anne. With their generous proportions, shady verandahs, and decorative windows, Queen Anne homes could be found across the country in all shapes and sizes; even small-town farmhouses like this Long Island residence often displayed the style.

Built in the late 1800s, the handsome house has recently found a new life as a comfortable eleven-room country home for an interior designer and her family. That transformation, how-ever, came only after nearly four years of hard labor, much of it undertaken by the designer herself. When the family found the house, it was derelict: "Most potential buyers would take one look at the kitchen and run the other way," she recalls. Yet, having grown up in a similar Victorian-era house, she still felt drawn to the old building. "In spite of its problems, it was welcoming, sunny, and cheerful—all the things I look for in a good house."

One major attraction for the family was the cool front porch, where the original turned posts and decorative latticework have been restored.

Continued

After years of neglect, the circa 1890 Long Island farmhouse above was restored to its original appearance. Among its period features is the wraparound verandah, right. Such porches were popular in the Victorian era, and were often furnished with comfortable rockers and wicker chairs.

The kitchen, right, is large enough to accommodate sitting and dining areas; the focal point is the fireplace, which has been refaced with Mexican tiles.

Nineteenth-century Stafford-shire figurines often depicted dogs; the spaniel, above, was one of the more popular sub-jects. Used as mantelpiece ornaments, such pieces were usually made in facing pairs.

The bedroom above features an elaborate 19th-century iron and brass bed that was found at a yard sale and restored.

Decorated with sisal matting and an assortment of comfortable old furniture (renewed with a fresh coat of white paint), the space has been transformed into an inviting outdoor room, much used in warm weather.

The relaxed look of the porch is continued in the interior, where walls were knocked down to produce larger, more open living spaces. A thirty-by-twenty-foot kitchen area was created by combining an existing kitchen, a butler's pantry, and a laundry porch. Here, the old wainscoting on the walls and ceiling was repainted, and a new pine floor was laid to replace the original, a lost cause beneath a layer of linoleum.

The casual furnishings found in the residence are mostly refurbished tag-sale finds, and include everything from a Victorian-era brass bed to inexpensive rag rugs. As a result, the house has a whimsical, personal look, and clearly reflects the pleasure that was taken in decorating it. Sometimes, the designer simply let a piece of furniture or a favorite textile inspire an idea for a room; the green-striped 1930s quilts in one bedroom, for example, suggested the soft color scheme that now predominates there. The same relaxed approach was taken throughout the house. "I didn't follow any one plan," says the designer. "I just wanted cheerful, pretty rooms."

In the guest bedroom, above, the colors in the circa 1930s quilts inspired the choices of wallcovering, framed prints, and rug.

QUILTS OF THE 1930S

In the early 1930s, a Gallup survey of major city newspapers in America revealed that their most popular features were the Sunday quilt columns. Quiltmaking had fallen from favor for a brief period around the turn of the century, but interest began to pick up after World War I, and by the thirties, quilt patterns were widely printed in newspapers and in ladies' magazines.

The reasons for the revival were many. During the Depression, a bedcover stitched from fabric scraps was an important symbol of thrift and industry. Moreover, quiltmaking was considered an antidote to the frantic atmosphere of the jazz age. "We hear so much about this 'jazz age' being hard on the nerves," wrote two quilters in 1935, declaring that quilting was "the ideal prescription. . . ."

Department stores also played a role in the quilt revival by promoting the needlecraft in order to sell yard goods. The quality of domestic cottons had been improving since World War I, and by the 1930s a wide selection of fabrics in bright, saturated colors were tempting needleworkers, who stitched them into striking quilts like those at right. While appliqué was also done, pieced patterns were favored. These included the popular Grandmother's Flower Garden, Dresden Plate, and Double Wedding Ring, as well as old favorites such as the Log Cabin, reinterpreted in the new, bright fabrics.

An Ohio Landmark

Known as Quaker Hill, this rambling clapboard residence—one of the earliest in southwestern Ohio—has been transformed into an elegant home by two dedicated, knowledgeable antiques collectors. They have spent some thirty years restoring the old farm-house and assembling the impressive collection of period furnishings that now fills it, and their ambitious preservation project has extended to all of the rooms in the building, which has been altered on many occasions over its lifetime.

The original part of the house, in fact, was a

much smaller dwelling, built by Judge John Ewing, one of the first settlers in the area. In 1797, Ewing migrated north from Kentucky with his wife and eight children, and began work that same year on his new farmhouse, a clapboarded timber-frame structure insulated with bricks

made on the site. An addition believed to have gone up by 1815 nearly doubled the size of the house; a second addition, built in the 1830s, provided a new kitchen and dining room in a "T" wing that is located behind the main section.

Descendants of the Ewings continued to live

Continued

Altered several times during the 19th and 20th centuries, the Ohio residence at left was begun in 1797 as a two-story, four-room homestead. Some of the later additions, such as the 1940s portico, have been retained.

The oak floors and walnut mantel in the living room, left, are original to the 18th-century section of the house. Among the furnishings from that period are a Queen Anne armchair with a vase-shaped splat, from the Hudson River Valley, and a William and Mary gate-leg table; the carpet is an antique Heriz.

Salvaged from a house in Massachusetts, the 18th-century corner cupboard above displays a collection of Historical Blue china.

in the house and to farm the property—which covered almost one thousand acres—throughout most of the 1800s. By the early 20th century, however, the structure had fallen into disrepair, and was being used as a tenant farm. A family bought the house in the 1940s, when the Ewing land was parceled out for development, and proceeded to modernize the interior, adding wall-to-wall carpeting, wallpaper, and a plate glass window. The pillared, colonial-style portico that runs across the façade was also added at that time.

For the current owners, who purchased the house some years later, renovation of the building meant reversing a number of these "improvements." Carpet was taken up to reveal the original hardwood floors, and wallpaper was removed to expose plaster walls. Fortunately, they found that many of the early architectural

features of the house—including hand-planed beaded-board paneling, mantelpieces, and chair rails—had been left untouched and only needed a bit of refurbishing. The six fireplaces, however, had been made smaller to accommodate standard dampers, and restoring them to their original dimensions was a bigger job.

The renovation effort extended not only to the individual architectural features of the old farm-house, but also to its character and quirks. "We accepted the wrinkles and sags," say the home-owners. "We like them—they're what makes the house homey." And while the owners were interested in accuracy, they were not averse to making some additions and changes of their own. In the living room, for example, they installed formal dentil molding and an antique hand-carved corner cupboard, both of which they felt were in

Continued

The bonnet-top Queen Anne highboy above just fits under the living room ceiling. Visible through the door is the old brick nogging used to insulate the house.

A set of Windsor chairs and an oversize pine hutch-table make practical furnishings for the keeping room kitchen, right. The English and American pewter is not only displayed, but also used.

Kettles made of copper, a superior heat conductor, were produced in America as early as the 1700s. Many, however, were imported from England, where the 19th-century piece above was crafted.

keeping with the look of an 18th-century home.

A more extensive modification involved raising the roof over the one-and-one-half-story kitchen and dining room wing, to create a second-story game room for the couple's two young sons. After the children had grown, the space was redecorated and is now divided into a sitting room and a "tavern" room. Woodwork

salvaged from an earlier house that was being torn down nearby was used to help blend these new rooms in with the rest of the house.

As the restoration and remodeling proceeded over the years, the homeowners were always adding to their collection of furnishings. "We felt that the house would be a perfect setting in which to display our antiques," say the collectors. While

Continued

An early-1800s English portrait hangs in the kitchen sitting area, above, where an old wagon seat is pulled up to the fireplace. A built-in cupboard in the dining room, right, is used to display a collection of 19th-century ironstone decorated with copper luster.

Among the antique textiles in the bedroom at right is a scarlet linsey-woolsey coverlet, made in 1824 by nineteen-year-old Elizabeth Northrup of Marcy, New York. Its excellent condition indicates that the piece was probably used only on special occasions.

both are Ohio natives, they have chosen to decorate their home primarily with pieces from New England; it was during a honeymoon trip to this region that their interest in period furnishings, especially Queen Anne pieces, was kindled. Throughout the house can be found the graceful vase-splat chairs and cabriole-leg highboys characteristic of that early-18th-century style. The owners have not restricted themselves to one look, however, and when a beautiful Sheraton tester bed or a more rustic painted Pennsylvania-German chest caught their eye, they mixed them in with their other pieces.

In addition to furniture, the couple are also interested in textiles, assembling a striking collection of richly colored antique Oriental rugs, and several 19th-century handwoven coverlets. Early tableware is another passion. Shelves and mantelpieces in almost every room display a selection of ironstone, Historical Blue china, or pewter; the pewter is a particularly appropriate addition, as an 1817 probate inventory of Judge Ewing's estate lists the ware among his household possessions.

A Sheraton butternut tester bed, dressed with a New York coverlet dated 1850, awaits guests in the bedroom at left. Furnished with 18th-century antiques, the upstairs sitting area, above, is used for entertaining. The door and mantel were salvaged from another house.

WHITE IRONSTONE

The fine, durable china known as ironstone first appeared in England in the early 1800s, after a 1794 tariff had raised the price of imported Chinese porcelains. Among the many potters who joined the effort to produce an affordable alternative was Charles Mason of Staffordshire, who in 1813 coined the term "ironstone" when he offered his new "Patent Ironstone China" for sale.

As its name was intended to suggest, ironstone—said to contain iron slag—was extremely strong, and sales of the practical wares produced by Mason and his competitors met with great success. Early pieces, which were marketed on both sides of the Atlantic, were decorated with glazed and transfer designs, but it was not until the mid-1800s that all-white ironstone like that shown at right was produced in quantity. Introduced to compete with inexpensive white porcelains that were then being exported from France to the States, white ironstone was specifically intended for American buyers. Shipped by the ton to this country, often as ballast, it became an immensely popular alternative to the excessively ornate porcelains that dominated the market at the time.

The white ironstone was sold in enormous table services comprising dozens of pieces. A set might include as many as seventy-two plates, which came in five sizes, as well as cups, gravy boats, platters, tureens (complete with trays and ladles), relish dishes, compotes, cookie and doughnut stands, covered cheese keeps, butter dishes, syrup dispensers, and muffin servers. Ironstone tea services, punch bowls, and chamber sets were also available.

To keep customers interested in purchasing the all-white pottery, many different patterns were produced; nearly three hundred have been identified to date, and there may be more. One of the earliest white ironstone designs is the simple, angular "Gothic" pattern introduced in 1842. Around the 1850s, more rounded, ornate forms with floral designs were offered, as well as pieces molded with wheat sheaf and corncob patterns inspired by the midwestern prairies, where increasing numbers of potential buyers were settling. In the 1870s, American potteries began to manufacture white ironstone, and both the imported and the domestic wares remained popular until the turn of the century.

The white ironstone wares at right were made in England in the mid-1800s, and display some of the many forms and patterns that were popular.

Farmhouse Living

When he first saw it, the potter who restored this Federal-period house on a former dairy farm in upstate New York was captivated by the view it afforded of the nearby Berkshire Hills, and by an old carriage barn on the site that could be converted into a studio. Having lived in New York City, he was also attracted by the seclusion—as well as by the gardening opportunities—that the seven-acre property offered.

The task of renovating the long-neglected 1830s house, however, was one for which the

The main section of the farmhouse at left was built in the 1830s; a smaller end wing, now containing the dining room and kitchen, was added later in the century, as was the Victorian entry porch.

homeowner was, admittedly, unprepared. When he purchased the building, it was structurally sound, but badly in need of a new roof. Moreover, the interior, which featured an unworkable kitchen and a 1950s-vintage decor, required considerable remodeling, not to mention an ex- tensive cosmetic overhaul. The challenge was so great, in fact, that, even with the help of a friend who was an interior designer, it took seven years' worth of hard work and careful planning to transform the farmhouse into a comfortable home—now complete with a hundred-foot-long

Continued

The decorative floor treatments in the hall and living room, above, show two variations on a checkerboard pattern; a trompe l'oeil painting of seed packets is a whimsical accent.

perennial garden that blooms from spring to fall.

"If I had known what I was getting into," says the owner, "I'm not sure I would have gotten into it." Indeed, each project seemed to be a time-consuming job unto itself. For example, three months were devoted just to sanding and refinishing the living room and entry hall floors—which were stripped of four layers of old paint, then refurbished with distinctive cream-and-taupe "tile" patterns.

Another, even more intensive, undertaking

Continued

A lighthearted floral theme distinguishes the decor of the living room, right, where paneling was freshened with cream-colored paint.

involved the complete overhaul of the kitchen, which is located in a late-19th-century addition to the main house. Here, three tiny rooms—a galley kitchen, a breakfast room, and a bathroom—were gutted to create a new fifteen-by-twenty-foot space. Rough-cut beams and the old barn siding that was used for the kitchen cabinets were washed with a cream color to keep the look rustic, yet light. The tulipwood plank floor was whitewashed, then studded with hand-forged, roundheaded nails to create a raised pattern. Multipaned French doors opening to a back terrace let in plenty of sunshine and offer views of the distant hills.

The casual furnishings used throughout the house include antiques, picked up at auctions or at local shops, mixed with some new pieces—including a rustic twig bed and a folk-art figure of a potter. Accessories such as rugs, baskets, decoys, and old quilts complete the simple country decor, which seems particularly well suited to the now-comfortable old farmhouse.

A small kitchen sink, above, is used to wash vegetables grown in the backyard garden. Kitchen staples are stored in glass jars, making it easy to tell when it is time for a refill.

Opened up with a cathedral ceiling, the kitchen, opposite, features a maple island fitted with both gas and electric cooktops; friends frequently pull up stools while the homeowner, an avid cook, prepares meals. Rough barn siding creates a rustic country look for the cupboards, while pink and white tiles and globe lighting fixtures were added as contemporary accents.

Furnishings in the bedroom at left include a handsome twig bed, and two quilts bought at auction. The floor covering is sisal; hooked and rag throw rugs add touches of color.

Of the few published works early Americans had in their homes, none—not even the Bible—was more indispensable than an almanac. Any farmer wanting to know how to graft trees, geld cattle, or get rid of rats, needed only to turn to the pages of this paperbound annual, a compendium of maps, calendars, astrological guides, agricultural tables, and all "Matters Curious, Useful and Entertaining."

Almanacs were among the earliest printed matter in America: the first press in the colonies was set up in 1638 in Cambridge, Massachusetts, and the second publication printed on it was William Peirce's almanac for the year 1639. Early volumes like Peirce's, called philomath almanacs, were essentially calendars peppered with lessons in history and assorted educational facts. Farmers' almanacs, which appeared by the middle of the century, continued this basic format, also providing tables and charts that detailed the movements of the sun, moon, and stars, and offering astrological and meteorological predictions. Such information was vital in helping farmers to tell time, forecast the weather, and plan their planting schedules.

In an effort to capture a broad readership, however, farmers' almanacs offered a heavy dose of humor—as well as verse, anecdotes, essays on famous people, and even romantic tales. Stagecoach schedules, lists of holidays, home remedies, recipes, and riddles were also included, along with all manner of advice,

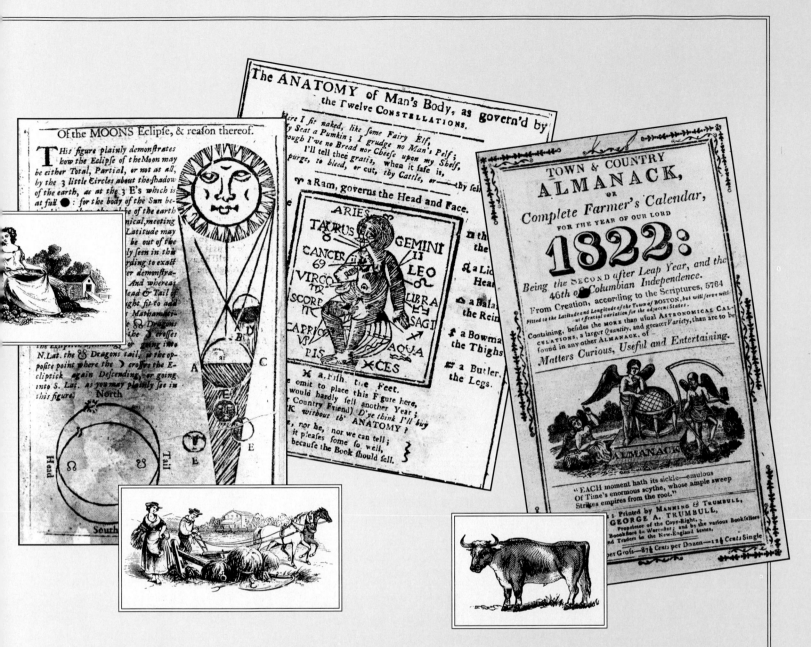

ranging from the sound to the dubious. A typically eccentric entry in one publication, for example, recommended planting beets only on moonless nights. Almanac contents were so broad, in fact, that the annuals were read not only by farmers, but by virtually everybody.

In the 17th and 18th centuries, more almanacs were published than all other books combined. Hundreds of different versions—remarkably similar in appearance and content—were produced until the late 1800s,

when improved communications reduced the need for the publications. Among the most popular of all almanacs was *The Farmer's Almanac,* founded in Boston in 1792 by Robert B. Thomas. A farmer and bookseller from a small Massachusetts town, Thomas built up one of the most successful almanac businesses of his, and all, time. After 1832, the word "Old" was inserted in the title; still produced today, *The Old Farmer's Almanac* is the oldest continuously published periodical in America.

As the covers and pages from the American farmers' almanacs above reveal, astrology was a primary subject of these all-purpose publications. Because the publishers took their illustrations from popular type-specimen books, the almanacs tended to have a similar look.

Country Conversions

recycling old buildings
for contemporary living

Buying an old barn, schoolhouse, tavern, or any other nonresidential building and turning it into a place to live is one way to be sure you have a home like no other. Part of the challenge in owning such a property lies in preserving its integrity and allowing the character of the building to shine through—while making the space itself comfortable to live in.

As the owners of the residences presented in this chapter are quick to point out, taking such a project from start to finish is hardly a simple process. Adapting an old building to a new use requires a certain amount of design ability (here, one home-owner was an architect, and another a designer), as well as time, flexibility, and financial resources. In many cases, a conversion can be more like building a house from the ground up. Yet, as each of these homes reveals, patience and hard work pay off, producing unusual residences that reflect the personal tastes of the families who live in them.

A gate-leg table serves for dining in a converted one-room schoolhouse.

The 19th-century bell above came from a one-room schoolhouse in Emmaus, Pennsylvania. It is slated for installation in the cupola of the old school at right, whose own bell was sold at auction years ago.

Schoolhouse Revival

Late one afternoon while driving through a small town near Zionsville, Pennsylvania, a young couple made a chance turn onto a country road. Following it to the top of a hill they came to a sudden stop: what they had found was the abandoned Powder Valley School, a late-19th-century one-room schoolhouse that had served that rural community from 1888 to 1950. Within the hour the pair had agreed to buy the stone structure from its owner, who lived on the adjoining property.

Long-time admirers of Pennsylvania's historic architecture, the couple had been looking for an old building, such as a barn, that they could convert into a house. "Unfortunately, we discovered that most barns were either too expensive or too far beyond repair for us to consider," says one of the owners, who is an architect.

The schoolhouse, on the other hand, was not only affordable, but also in relatively sound condition. Converting the old structure to residential use, however, did present challenges of its own. It was particularly important to the couple, for example, to preserve the "schoolhouse character" that had originally attracted them to the building. Thus, to avoid dividing the one-room interior into smaller spaces, a two-story wing—for a kitchen, bedrooms, and baths—was added on in back; the old schoolroom, left much as it

Continued

Remodeled as a residence, the 1888 Powder Valley
School, left, gained an unobtrusive frame addition.
The simple lines of the old stone building were
intentionally echoed in the new wing.

A new cast-iron stove, above, replaces the original coal-burning stove that once heated the old schoolhouse.

had always been, now serves handily as an open living room and dining area.

The couple began their restoration and remodeling project by removing the stucco on the exterior of the schoolhouse in order to uncover the natural stone that was underneath; the task proved to be an especially grueling one, requiring two weeks of sandblasting. Then, it was necessary to rebuild and shingle the old roof, which was badly deteriorated.

Fortunately, it was possible to retain some early features of the structure as well. The fir

Continued

The door and window cut through the end wall of the living and dining area, opposite, connect the old classroom to a new addition built to house the kitchen, bedrooms, and baths.

rafters, for example, remained in good condition, and when the classroom's cracked plaster ceiling was taken down, the couple decided to leave the roofing framework exposed to create a cathedral ceiling in the spacious room. Exposing the original stonework on the gable wall contributed to the striking effect of the space, while ribbed wainscoting, a cast-iron stove, and a few old desks help to evoke a schoolroom spirit of days gone by.

By contrast, the rear wing was planned to have an intentionally newer feel, so it would not compete with the historic structure that it adjoins. The high ceiling in the kitchen was designed to echo the lofty lines of the schoolroom, however, creating an easy transition between the old and new sections of the house.

In all, the imaginative conversion from abandoned schoolhouse to updated residence took seven months of nonstop work. Still, the homeowners consider the project to have been more than worth the effort; not only did they create a comfortable home, they also gave new life to a proud old building.

A large, open interior window brings extra light into the master bedroom, above, while the smaller exterior window offers a glimpse of the bell cupola.

In the kitchen, opposite, country and high-tech styles are combined. Cherry was used for cabinets and shelf facings, while stainless steel was chosen for the countertops. The graphic checkerboard floor is made of long-wearing, resilient tile.

The Country Schoolhouse

Throughout the 19th century, one-room public schools were the mainstay of American education. The image of the little red schoolhouse, however, is largely a folk myth, as early schools in most rural villages were built with whatever materials were at hand—logs, sod, even branches—and were seldom painted at all. As funds became available, such primitive structures would be replaced by more substantial buildings, but even these were painted white more often than red.

In any case, a presentable façade was desirable, since in many small towns the school was a source of pride: a community with a school, it was felt, was a community with a future. Nevertheless, 19th-century schoolhouses, where the students generally ranged in age from six to eighteen, were frequently overcrowded, ill-equipped, badly lit, and poorly ventilated. For the most part, the quality of schooling was determined by the ability of the teachers—many of whom were only about sixteen years old themselves. In the worst circumstances, the education provided was dismal. It could also be excellent, since the single classroom setup allowed students to advance in a subject whenever they were ready; capable older students could also learn by helping to teach the younger pupils.

A typical school day ran from eight o'clock until four o'clock. The three most important subjects—reading, writing, and arithmetic—were taught in the morning, and were followed, perhaps, by grammar and geography in the afternoon. Generally, the older students studied or worked on slates at their desks while the younger ones were called forward, one at a time, to recite their lessons from memory or to work sums on a blackboard. Then the older pupils came forth while the younger ones studied. Spontaneity was not tolerated in the classroom until the late 1800s, and children typically heard the same lessons many times over; consequently, it was not uncommon for eleven- and twelve-year-olds to master the same material as boys and girls who were as many as three years older.

The daily routine of recitation and memorization was interrupted at noon with an hour-long break for lunch (which was brought from home in a tin pail) and, if time allowed, recess. There were no playgrounds, but children could run and tumble outdoors or engage in organized games, such as snap-the-whip or kick-the-can, until the bell called them back to class.

For many students, the best part of school was the special challenge presented by the weekly spelling bee. The children stood while the teacher assigned increasingly complex spelling words to each. Eventually only the victor would remain standing: it was one of the few chances for a child to take the spotlight in a one-room school.

Finer schoolhouses, such as this one in East Lansing, New York, had separate entries for boys and girls. A flag was raised at the start of the day.

In 1907, when these pupils attended class in New York State, one-room schools still served more than half of all schoolchildren in America.

This little girl prepares to recite her lessons in 1901; since books were scarce, memorization and recitation were standard in rural schools.

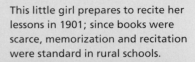

In Texas and Oklahoma, "brush arbor" schools like this one provided temporary classrooms while permanent schoolhouses were being built.

Teachers in rural schools looked forward to their few chances to meet and share ideas. This group posed in Leadville, Colorado, in 1901.

As was typical in mountainous areas, where travel could be difficult in wintertime, this Virginia school held summer sessions.

Lacking both timber and stone, settlers on the Great Plains used prairie sod to construct buildings like this 19th-century Nebraska schoolhouse.

69

New Life for an Old Barn

At first glance, this weekend house near Woodstock, New York, still looks very much like the horse barn that it was designed to be in the 1870s. On one side of the weathered building, however, a forty-foot-high window spanning three stories suggests the dramatic changes that were made as the old barn was transformed into a spacious country home.

When a New York City couple bought the 150-acre property several years ago, the barn was still home to eight horses—as well as to a family of raccoons—but the floorboards were

Continued

When the hillside house above, in New York State, was created from a 19th-century barn, the old structure gained a steeper roof; the small wing houses a mudroom.

A mix of new and old distinguishes the open living and sleeping areas, left, where weathered steel beams and recycled pine posts were left exposed.

rotting and the roof was caving in. Initially, the owners considered tearing down the structure and putting up an entirely new house. Then, an architect who saw beyond its dilapidated state convinced them that—with considerable help—the barn could become exactly the kind of home they had in mind. "He showed us that an old barn offers wonderful qualities of space and light that can inspire an interesting design," says one of the owners. "But taking on this kind of project does mean changing the traditional concept of what a house should look like."

Before the new house could emerge, extensive work was necessary. First, the walls and roof were stripped back to their skeletons, then carefully reframed by hand using traditional joinery techniques. While this attention to historical detail reveals a concern for preserving the structural integrity of the old building, the architect was equally interested in creating some surprises. In areas where the barn's old poured-concrete floors were still serviceable, the concrete was simply left in place and sealed with polyurethane. In parts of the building where it was not possible to salvage the existing floors, thick mahogany "truck flooring," normally used to line

Continued

In the dining area, above, poured concrete flooring was left in place and sealed with polyurethane to protect it from moisture and to make cleaning easier.

In the living area, opposite, hand-hewn timbers set off "gallery" space for effective displays of wire rug beaters and old farm tools, including rakes and a pitchfork. The rustic Adirondack-style furnishings are well-suited to the converted barn.

Recycled materials in the sleeping balcony, above, include mahogany "truck flooring," and chimney stones, which came from an old wall on the property.

truck trailers, was laid down and also given a coat of polyurethane. Steel beams were left outdoors to weather slightly, then sealed to prevent further rust. They come close to matching the barn's pine beams in color, but also add a high-tech look of their own when used as frames for windows, or as supports for staircases and floors.

To emphasize the loftlike feeling, the architect designed a cathedral ceiling and kept the spaces open. Conceived as oversize balconies, the upper stories can be used as bedrooms or as extra living areas. The kitchen, living room, and din-

ing areas on the main floor are also open, for a free flow of traffic and conversation.

The unstructured floor plan, which allows views of woods or rolling farmland from every window, is well-suited to this casual country home, where a clean, contemporary look seems in perfect harmony with the rustic character inherent in the old barn. The architectural design is complemented by a collection of Adirondack-style furnishings, while old farm tools and rug beaters have been used to create graphic displays against the white walls.

The steep pitch of the roof is especially evident in the master bedroom, opposite, where the rafters and roof boards were left exposed. Forming a geometric pattern, a series of simple windows punctuates the gable wall and opens up dramatic views of the New York countryside.

AMERICAN BARNS

For anyone who enjoys traveling down country roads, old barns are among the best-loved sights in the American landscape. While many of these venerable symbols of the nation's agricultural heritage are no longer used for their original purposes, their straightforward craftsmanship, economical designs, and simple beauty still capture the American imagination.

Often built by community effort in neighborhood "barn raisings," American barns like those at right display countless designs, many of which are based on European precedents. However, the concept of a separate barn—detached from the house and used for both storing hay and sheltering livestock—developed in this country. In the early colonial settlements, the detached barns were typically situated close to the road so that the world could see that a family's farm was in good order. But even when a barn was located in a less prominent place, it remained a source of pride to the farmer, who had built the structure to last well beyond his own lifetime.

A Tavern Reborn

Carefully restored, the fieldstone house above looks much the way it did when it was operated as an inn in the 18th and early 19th centuries.

No one knows exactly when the stone house shown on these pages was built, but town records reveal that by 1761 its owners were petitioning for an innkeeper's license. For the next sixty years, the building served the farming communities around Parsley's Ferry, New Jersey, as an inn and tavern.

During the 1800s, the tavern was enlarged and remodeled several times. In the early dec-ades of the century, presumably as business flourished, a two-story stone wing was added to the rear, and a single-story wooden section, hous-ing a kitchen, was attached to one end. By the turn of the century, the building had been con-verted for use as a private home, gaining a stuc-coed exterior finish, a fashionable front porch, and new windows, as well as updated paneling and woodwork on the interior walls.

Interested in returning the house to its earlier appearance, the designer who was responsible for its recent restoration found that many original elements still existed; instead of being destroyed, they had simply been obscured by later alterations. Removing the 19th-century stucco, for example, revealed the fieldstone, or "rubblestone," masonry typical of houses along the Delaware River in this part of rural New Jersey.

Although the mud-and-lime mortar was still intact, the designer took the extra precaution of repointing the stonework with cement to protect the building against moisture damage.

Along the way, some surprises were also encountered. "Restoring an early building involves a fair amount of detective work," comments this veteran of numerous major restorations. "As you peel back layers, you discover clues

Continued

Above, the small, clapboard 19th-century addition to the building originally housed a kitchen and still serves that purpose today.

79

to what existed previously," he adds, stressing that it is important to work with carpenters and masons who take the time to notice details and use them as guides. For example, when the Victorian porch, which was badly deteriorated, was torn down, traces were found of the early pent roof that had run between the first and second stories on the front façade; the decision was made to reconstruct it. And when the two-over-two Victorian-era windows were removed, the old nail holes that were uncovered indicated that the house originally had nine-over-six win-

Continued

A small stenciled motif brings subtle color to the plaster walls in the dining room, where the original nine-over-six windows and paneled shutters have been carefully reproduced. Antique furnishings include a 19th-century deacon's bench, left, and a tall-case clock, above, made in the 1700s.

The attractive kitchen display above includes two folk-art "cow portraits," English reproductions of 19th-century American primitive paintings.

dows, as well as interior shutters. These, too, were restored.

Despite his interest in accuracy, however, the designer was not trying to achieve a literal reconstruction. "Anyone getting involved in a project like this has got to decide just how much of a purist he wants to be," he explains. "I wanted to return the house to the way it might have looked when it was a tavern, but I also wanted a house that would be comfortable to live in."

Thus, when creating a new kitchen and informal dining area in the wood-frame wing, he was willing to add sliding glass doors; while these may not be "historical," they opened the

Continued

Designed with small panes for an old-fashioned look, sliding glass doors let light into the kitchen dining area, right, where reproduction English and American folk art enhances a country feeling.

After the Revolution, the bald eagle became America's national symbol, as well as a popular folk-art motif. The painted wooden eagle above is one of many crafted by the Pennsylvania carver Wilhelm Schimmel in the late 19th century.

In the living room, above, the plaster walls were painted brick red and stenciled to suggest the look of wallpaper.

room to views of the surrounding cornfields. Moreover, their small-pane design is consistent with the window style throughout the house.

Similarly, any modernizations were introduced as discreetly as possible. When the Victorian woodwork was removed from the parlor and the keeping room—now both used as living rooms—the designer discovered that the original plaster walls were still intact and in relatively good condition. He decided to keep them, but because the plaster had been applied directly to the masonry, the walls could not be insulated.

The solution was to insulate the floors and the ceilings instead. A radiant-heat system, also installed in the ceiling, eliminated the need for floor-level heat registers.

As the finished project shows, all of the work done in the home was aimed at maintaining the feeling of a late-18th-century building while establishing a sense of modern comfort. "The most important thing in any restoration is to find the right balance between old and new," comments the designer. "And when you find it—consider the job finished."

The 18th-century fireplace and mantelpiece in the keeping room, above, are original to the house.

TAVERN DRINKS

Of all the activities that took place in a colonial tavern, drinking, a "traditional rite, rooted in custom and sanctioned by practice," was by far the most popular. Alcohol was considered to be good for one's health; it helped to ease the burden of hard labor, it was warming in winter and cooling in summer, and it was often more potable than water. Drinking was also an extremely important social activity in colonial times, and sharing a glass in the local tavern was a symbol of good fellowship.

Although colonial Americans imbibed more hard cider than any other alcoholic beverage, rum—both imported and domestic—was the most popular distilled liquor sold in taverns. Establishments catering to the working classes sometimes served rum only; referred to as rum ordinaries, these places were of somewhat dubious repute. Often, the rum was consumed "plain," but it might be mixed with an equal amount of water to make a "sling." Diluting the rum with a higher proportion of water (three parts) produced "grog."

In the more respectable taverns, any number of libations were available to those who could afford them. Corn and rye liquors, apple, peach and cherry brandies, and various types of beers all had their loyal followers. Wine was popular mainly in urban areas; German Rhine wines were called hock, and white Spanish and Canary Island wines were known as sack. When sweet wine was mixed with milk or cream, sugar, and sometimes spices, and whipped to a froth, the result was a "syllabub."

Perhaps the most popular mixed beverage sold in better taverns, however, was punch, which was derived from an Indian concoction called *panch*. The word, meaning "five" in Hindi, refers to the number of principal ingredients (spirits, fruit juice, sugar, water, and spices) that were found in this exotic drink. Among the many colonial variations were "sower," or citrus, punch, milk and brandy punches, and wine punch, which was also called sangaree. Punches were usually served warm and in a large bowl; each imbiber took a drink directly from the punch bowl, then passed it on.

Toasting was commonplace in most taverns. Some drinks were served in thick-bottomed glass vessels called firing glasses, and after a popular toast was given, the glass would be rapped sharply on a table to produce a noise that sounded like a musket firing—making for a loud, but presumably convivial, gathering.

A variety of ingredients, such as pears, sugar, spices, and, of course, liquor, were used for making the punches and other popular drinks that were served in colonial taverns.

THREE

Cabin Living

*rustic houses that
recall the past*

The log cabin was introduced to this country by Swedish homesteaders who began settling along the Delaware River in the 1630s. By the time of the Revolution, it had become the shelter of choice for many frontiersmen, and remained so until the late 19th century; the thick wood walls provided natural insulation, keeping the interior warm in winter and cool in summer.

It is not surprising, then, that even today enterprising homeowners still seek out log cabins for contemporary living. The houses featured in this chapter incorporate cabins that were taken down and moved to their present sites because their owners found this to be an economical means of getting more living space. One is a small 1840s stone house in Texas to which a long cabin has been added; the other is an amalgam of three 19th-century Tennessee cabins. After careful restoration, these historic dwellings have been filled with simple regional antiques and handmade crafts to achieve a comfortable, lived-in look that suits their rustic roots.

A hooked rug displayed on the wall reflects the casual spirit of a Tennessee cabin.

A Texas Past

Moved from the German settlement of New Braunfels, Texas, the log cabin section of the house, above, features a roof design that originated in Europe; the steep slope was intended to shed snow.

In the mid-19th century, the hill country of southwestern Texas was settled by hundreds of French, German, and Alsatian immigrants, whose simple pioneer cabins can still be found in many communities there. This handsome residence in Castroville is actually made up of two such dwellings: one is a stucco-covered stone house built in the 1840s by an Alsatian named P. F. Pingenot, and the other is a 19th-century log cabin that was recently moved to the Castroville site and incorporated as an addition.

The ambitious restoration and remodeling project began with Pingenot's small, steep-roofed stone house, which captured the imagination of the current owners in spite of the fact that its most interesting architectural features were buried beneath layers of siding, plasterboard, and linoleum. "We had always wanted to live in a historic Texas home," explains one of the homeowners, "and when we saw this house,

Continued

The living room, opposite, is located in the stone house built by P. F. Pingenot in the 1840s; the oak beams and flagstone floor were uncovered during restoration. Regional furnishings include a Biedermeier-style settee and 19th-century stoneware from the Wilson pottery, near Seguin, Texas.

The large food safe in the living room, above, holds ceramics that are primarily the work of William Meyer, a German potter who emigrated to Texas in the 1880s.

we felt sure that we had found one." Indeed, as the original fieldstone-and-stucco façade, half-timbered framework, oak beams, and flagstone floors were gradually uncovered, that historic house emerged.

For all its character and history, however, the dwelling offered less than seven hundred square feet in floor area. The innovative solution to the space problem was the addition of the trans-planted two-room log cabin; characterized by the same rugged feeling as the Pingenot house, this structure had been built in the mid-1800s in the nearby German settlement of New Braunfels. A long half-timbered passageway was created to

join the stone and log buildings, which feature similar rooflines. To further blend the two house sections, some of the log walls were partially stuccoed to suggest the look of half-timbering.

Also unifying the appearance of the house are the antique furnishings used throughout the rooms. The extensive selection represents more than thirty years of collecting by the couple, who have found many prized pieces in second-hand shops and on leisurely back-road travels. "When we first started collecting, some people considered these pieces to be junk and were hap-py to be rid of them," says one of the home-owners. "We were happy to oblige them."

Continued

The bedroom at left is located in what was originally the kitchen of the Pingenot house; the outline of the former cooking fireplace is still visible behind the bed.

The tall pine food safe in the kitchen, right, was found in another old Texas house, where it had literally been holding up the roof. A hickory basket filled with hand-blown glass eggs—which were used in hens' nests to encourage egg pro-duction—and stoneware butter churns from Atascosa County stand near the foot of the cupboard.

*The cozy dining area at left
is furnished with a mid-19th-
century cypress-and-pine
table found in a chicken yard;
the German Biedermeier-
style chairs were made
in Texas.*

The collection is distinguished by many regionally made furnishings. Several of these feature the gracefully curved lines of the style now known as Biedermeier, which was fashionable in central Europe during the early 1800s and prevalent in the Germanic settlements of 19th-century Texas. Notable are two pine food safes; with their massive proportions and heavy cornices, these cupboards resemble the German *schrank,* or wardrobe, in design, and were probably crafted locally by German immigrants. Enhancing the European flavor are a number of 18th-century copper cooking molds, including some that were brought from France. Hand-pegged tables and chairs of native pine and cypress add rustic accents.

Above, exposed timbers and a pine wall shelf offer display space for a collection of copper molds.

The comfortable sitting area opposite is dominated by a fireplace and hearth, which the homeowners had made of fieldstone brought to Castroville from Fredericksburg, Texas. The antique cooking utensils include ladles, dippers, and cooking pots.

MINIATURE LOG CABINS

Few people born in the 20th century actually grew up in log cabins, but the rustic dwellings have a particular appeal for both children and adults as evocative symbols of America's pioneer past.

Not surprisingly, log cabins are often featured in American folk crafts and art. The miniature cabins at left, dating from about 1900 to the 1930s, were made in Pennsylvania and states south, including Tennessee and Georgia, where log cabins were once familiar sights.

These miniatures, all handcrafted, are of two different types. The tiniest cabins were sold earlier in this century at roadside souvenir shops in mountain towns and at tourist areas. Such pieces can be quite similar in appearance, since an artisan would simply repeat a successful design in order to hasten assembly and keep a ready supply on hand.

In contrast, the larger cabins, all distinctly different, were never intended for sale. Made by fathers and grandfathers for their own families, they were used once a year in miniature villages, set up under Christmas trees. Some are decorated with snow on the roofs, and others have holes in the bottom for a tree light. While such cabins were crafted with twigs, scraps of lumber, and bits of glass—whatever materials were found around the yard and house—they nevertheless exhibit the lavish attention paid to details: "logs" are carefully notched, roofs are clad with scaled-down shingles, and chimneys are built of tiny "bricks."

Log Cabin
Pleasures

Two Tennessee log cabins were joined together to form the front section of the house, above.

Located on a wooded ridge in rural northeastern Tennessee, this rambling log residence was constructed from three 19th-century cabins, as well as "spare parts" salvaged from several others. It is home to two long-time collectors whose passion for regional furniture and folk art sent them looking for a house that was large enough to accommodate all of their belongings.

"We found that the most economical way to get the space we needed for both our family and our furniture was to rebuild log houses—and do most of the work ourselves," says one of the owners. The couple's adventure began with frequent trips around the state, as they searched for the right "components." In Morgan County, they found a small Civil War-era cabin, which proved suitable for a living room, and in Campbell County, a four-room cabin—with the date 1838 carved into some of its logs—which they

turned into bedrooms. A third cabin was discovered in Union County; previously a hay and cattle shed, it is now joined to the other two buildings and serves handily as a kitchen.

Connecting the three different buildings, however, was only a small part of a project that involved considerable preparation work. Before the bedroom cabin could be moved to its new location, for example, it was necessary to take off the layers of siding and plasterboard that virtually concealed its log structure. After the buildings were stripped of such modern "amenities," each cabin was then taken down piece by piece, the parts numbered for reassembly, and the logs carefully cleaned and repaired where needed.

When it came time to rebuild and combine the cabins, the homeowners decided to make practicality, rather than strict historical accuracy, a priority. To that end, their own improvements

Continued

The kitchen wing, above, extends from the rear of the house. The chimneys were built from recycled stone and brick.

included insulated windows and a new roof of durable cedar shakes. Whenever possible, however, the owners did try to maintain the original integrity of the three structures, leaving the hand-hewn logs exposed and making sure that any added elements were compatible with the early features. Old heart pine joists, for example, were hand-planed to make floorboards, while tongue-and-groove pine doors were reproduced from an original example, then fitted with hand-forged iron latches and hinges.

The finished house now brims with an imag-

Continued

The banjo in the hall, above, was crafted from pie tins. More homemade instruments are displayed in the living room, right, where a collection of Appalachian and Cherokee baskets is also found.

inative collection of furniture and handcrafts from Virginia, North Carolina, and eastern Tennessee. "It was a long time before factory-made goods first reached Appalachia, so people had to make their own things," says one home-owner. "Their household furnishings have a simplicity and a practicality that I find very appealing." Among her special interests are homemade Appalachian musical instruments and baskets; representing long-standing craft traditions of the region, these seem particularly appropriate additions to a Tennessee log cabin.

Old hand-formed bricks—some bearing their makers' fingerprints—were used to build the fireplace in the kitchen wing, left.

Above, butcher-block counters blend in with the rustic look of the kitchen, where the log walls and beams were left exposed.

*Among the furnishings in
the bedroom at left is a hand-
pegged poplar rope bed, made
in Virginia in the 1800s; the
pine table, bearing its original red paint, is a mid-19th-
century North Carolina piece.
An old fiddle case, hand-
painted in the 1800s, sits
on the blanket chest.*

APPALACHIAN BASKETS

Mac McCarter of Tennessee, with a white oak rib basket he crafted; c. 1930.

The form of the split basket below is unusual: the square shape suggested by the base becomes a circle at the rim. The "hole" handles are typical of Appalachian split baskets.

The southern highlands region of Appalachia is home to a tradition of basketmaking that extends back to the 1700s, when homesteaders began settling in the area. The pioneers and their descendants lived an isolated life and had to craft most of their own belongings. Although self-sufficiency is no longer a necessity in Appalachia, the techniques of basketweaving have passed down through the generations unchanged.

The preferred material for Appalachian baskets has long been white oak, which is strong, flexible, and easy to handle. White oak baskets can be divided into three traditional types: split, rib, and rod. Split baskets are made by interlacing flat strips, or "splits," into one integral form; the shape of the base usually dictates the shape of the basket.

By contrast, a rib basket is formed around a framework: the long splits used to lash the intersecting rim and handle together are laced around "ribs," which are inserted into the wrapping to provide structure.

Rod baskets, less common than split or rib baskets, are made with long splits, which are rounded to create "rods"; the rods are then woven into various patterns, creating particularly durable baskets.

The sampling of Appalachian baskets at right represents all three traditional types, and includes both contemporary and vintage 20th-century pieces.

The large, durable field basket at left displays the tight weave and "roped" handles often found in rodwork pieces made in the Shenandoah Valley of Virginia.

The fan-shaped design of the rib basket above was adapted from the more traditional rectangular form. The dark band was created with heartwood splits.

Lobed rib baskets like the West Virginia piece above are often called "buttocks," "fanny," or "melon" baskets. The decorative rim is edged with a round rib.

Oak rod baskets are always round or oval in shape. The two examples at left are from Ohio; bands of colored rods were worked into the weave of the larger basket as decoration.

The eight-inch-tall split basket above, which was probably made in Virginia's Shenandoah Valley, is a miniature version of a type used to store bedding feathers.

Country in the City

*a town house and an apartment
showcase country decor*

Having a "country house" in the middle of a city is wishful thinking for most urban dwellers. Yet more and more people are turning that wish into a reality by renovating and decorating old town houses, or by furnishing their apartments in country style. Even though an apartment might have white walls and no view of rolling hills, it can still be "country."

That was clear to the two New Yorkers who decorated the homes shown on the following pages. Each faced a different challenge in creating an individual look. The designer who purchased an 1856 town house knew she wanted a country decor that would suit the 19th-century interior of her brownstone. Before she could begin furnishing it, however, she had to undertake major renovation work to return the residence to its earlier splendor. Once that was accomplished, she filled her rooms with both elegant and primitive antiques. For the owner of a prewar apartment, the mission was to create an environment that suited her eclectic collection of country pieces. Through judicious use of color and clever furniture arrangements, she has transformed what might have been a cold city space into a welcoming haven.

Eclectic country furnishings distinguish this apartment dining room.

A Country Town House

The stately New York City town house above, built in 1856, still has its original paneled front door, cast-iron railings, and gate.

This mid-19th-century town house in Manhattan is the unexpected location for a country-style home. The owner, a designer and long-time collector who also sells antiques from her brownstone, was determined to create a friendly, relaxed retreat from the hectic city around her. She specifically chose this three-story town house—built in 1856 and therefore simpler in style than the many later Victorian-era residences in New York City—because it would

Continued

Housewares and cooking utensils from the 18th and 19th centuries are displayed in the front room at right, which doubles as an antiques shop.

be compatible with the early American look she wanted. Yet in remodeling and furnishing it, she was careful to keep the decor harmonious with the structure. "This house was built 'correctly,' with tasteful details such as curving staircases and plaster moldings," she explains. "So I felt it was important not to decorate so informally that

Continued

Above, an 18th-century Welsh dresser is used to display a collection of 19th-century English glassware.

Reproduction wallpaper and a molded chair rail were added to the redecorated dining room, left; the marble fireplace is original.

A handmade reproduction Chippendale sofa, an 18th-century English chimney glass, and a Queen Anne walnut slant-front desk contribute to the elegant look of the second-floor parlor, above.

the details would seem out of place—or so elegantly that I couldn't enjoy living here."

The decor, which the owner describes as "high country," incorporates such sophisticated furnishings as a burl-walnut dining set, Oriental rugs, and satin swag draperies, contrasted with Windsor chairs and other more traditional country pieces. In addition to forming an interesting mix of styles, the furnishings represent a variety of provenances and periods. There are pieces from

England as well as from New England and Pennsylvania, and the antiques range in date from the early 18th century, when the Queen Anne style came into fashion, to the eclectic decades of the late 1800s.

Before the brownstone could be furnished, however, considerable renovation work was needed. Over time, the building had been neglected, and its most desirable features—including eight fireplaces and inlaid hardwood floors—

Continued

A coat of paint was used to renew and lighten the parlor paneling opposite, which dates to the 1920s. A border of English delft floral-motif tiles from the 1720s was added to complement the fine molding detail surrounding the fireplace.

While most 19th-century inkwells were made of pottery or glass, the piece above is of tin, a less expensive alternative. Ink was stored in a master bottle, then transferred to the well, which would be used as a reservoir for dipping the pen.

were hardly being shown to advantage. Indeed, the house was in such a state of general disrepair that, says the owner, "only a person with vision could have recognized its potential."

Years of experience and a practiced eye proved instrumental in exploiting that potential during the rehabilitation, which involved numerous decisions about what to save and what to change. Some features, such as the crumbling plaster crown moldings that adorned many of the rooms, were carefully restored to their original state. Others, however, were altered to suit particular needs. Stained pine paneling in the parlor, for example, made this north-facing room so dark that the homeowner deemed it appropriate to paint over the wood with a light color. Elsewhere in the town house, white plaster walls were covered with floral-patterned wallpaper to add more color to the rooms. Because all such changes were carefully weighed by the owner, the result is an elegant city home with all the comfort of one in the country.

Chosen for its stencil-like pattern and soft colors, a reproduction colonial wallcovering was used to
paper the master bedroom. Cheerful accessories include the late-19th-century Star of Bethlehem quilt
on the tester bed, left, and the paper-covered hatbox and bandbox on the blanket chest, above.

DUTCH WALL TILES

Known for their fine craftsmanship, the Dutch are justifiably famous for their ceramic wares, especially their ornamental wall tiles of tin-glazed earthenware. Beginning in the early 17th century, Dutch tiles were exported the world over to great acclaim. Antique tiles are now relatively hard to come by, but new Dutch wall tiles like those at right are still produced in the Netherlands, where this national craft tradition has continued largely unchanged.

Although floor tiles had been made earlier, the Dutch wall tile industry started to develop around 1580, when the Netherlands was entering a time of great prosperity. Wall tiles were introduced as tile makers looked for a way to develop a market among a fast-growing population of well-to-do burghers. Favored for hallways, kitchens, and fireplace facings, the decorative glazed tiles were not only easy to keep clean, but provided a welcome solution to the problem of damp walls, which was widespread in the country's waterbound cities. Business thrived, and by the mid-1600s, the cities of Delft, Amsterdam, Haarlem, and Rotterdam had become important tile centers.

Initially, Dutch wall tiles were coarse and somewhat gaudy in appearance, reflecting the influence of Spanish and Italian polychrome majolica. When blue-and-white Chinese porcelain was imported to Holland beginning in the 1620s, tile makers started to emulate the look of this far more delicate ceramic ware, developing an improved clay mixture and turning to realistic motifs in a cobalt glaze. By the late 1600s some makers were using manganese purple in addition to cobalt blue, and around the beginning of the 1700s, the market for pictorial polychrome designs picked up.

The patterns depicted a wide range of subjects, including flowers, children at play, fishermen, ships at sea, portraits of royalty, and fantastic creatures such as sea serpents. Most tiles had a central image—sometimes framed by a lozenge, circle, or other geometric design. The corners on such pieces were also decorated, often with intersecting lines or tiny sprig motifs; when four tiles were laid in a square, the abutting corners formed a pattern. Other tiles featured only part of a picture, and were designed so that a certain number could be grouped together to create a large composition. These "wall paintings," which were often surrounded by border tiles, provided inexpensive decoration for householders who could not afford painted artworks.

The pieces at right display some of the many decorative themes that have been featured on Dutch wall tiles for centuries.

An Eclectic Apartment

The ornately carved door surround on the 1929 apartment house above is indicative of the fine stonework found on many prewar buildings in New York City.

Home to a clothing designer who appreciates a certain quirkiness in design, this 1929 apartment in New York City is a showcase for her own far-ranging tastes, rather than a study in any single country decorating style.

Each room exhibits an imaginative combination of furnishings and collectibles from various continents and time periods, and the owner gathered many of the pieces before she ever knew she would be living in the apartment. Once she

Continued

The eclectic living room furnishings, right, include an Empire sofa, a 1920s Chinese rug, and papier-mâché storks, once used in store displays.

The earthenware vase above,
decorated with a frond of
fuchsia blossoms, was made
by the Roseville Pottery Company of Zanesville, Ohio,
in 1938; such floral patterns
were among the firm's most
popular designs.

found the rambling space, complete with the ornate moldings and high ceilings that characterize many of the city's prewar buildings, she simply kept rearranging her possessions until they looked "right." Even today, the rooms continue to be works-in-progress, as pieces are added or as old favorites are moved to different spots. "The house is a mishmash," she admits, "but if you have a good eye and consistent taste, everything will work together somehow."

The success of the decor depends in part on a skillful use of color. Walls and ceilings are painted in high-gloss shades of rose, peach, or mint green, as backdrops for vividly hued furnishings and accessories. These include such varied pieces as an Empire sofa, a mid-19th-century country French armoire, and twig stands, as well as the whimsical array of ceramic dishware, vases, and salt and pepper shakers on display in the kitchen. By mixing—and constantly remixing—her diverse pieces, the owner has ensured a fresh, spontaneous look for her home.

Kitchen shelves, above, provide display space for favorite postcards and a collection of vases from early-20th-century American potteries.

The original 1920s cabinetry in the kitchen, opposite—including the glass doors—was found painted over. The doors were later stripped and waxed and the cabinet interiors painted a peach color to make an effective backdrop for assorted pottery pieces.

A floral-motif wallpaper with a black background sets a handsome yet feminine tone for the bedroom, right. The look is accented by a lace curtain found at a Paris flea market, a colorful old comforter, and a collection of throw pillows received as gifts.

The calla lily vase above is one in a series of blossom-shaped flower holders manufactured in the mid-1900s by the Nelson McCoy Pottery Works of Roseville, Ohio. The relatively wide availability of such vases makes them appealing to collectors.

MAKING A RUFFLED PILLOW

Pillows made with pretty fabric and trimmed with ribbon or lace can add a personal touch to your decor. You can buy ready-made pillow forms in various sizes, and mix and match fabrics, patterns, and colors as you like.

Square pillow forms, which are called for here, come in sizes from 12 to 30 inches, with fills of polyester fiber, cotton, or feathers. A sturdy fabric such as chintz is recommended for the covering; for the ruffle, use double-faced taffeta, satin, or grosgrain ribbon, or lace edging. This trim should be 2½ to 4 inches wide (the finished ruffle will be ½ inch narrower than the initial width).

If you are using ribbon, buy enough to measure two times the perimeter of the form. If you are using lace, which has less body than ribbon and has to be gathered more to achieve fullness, you will need a length measuring three times the perimeter of the form.

MATERIALS

- Square pillow form in size desired
- Sturdy fabric (enough to cover pillow form generously)
- Ribbon or lace for trim (for type and amount, see information at left)
- Dressmakers' pins

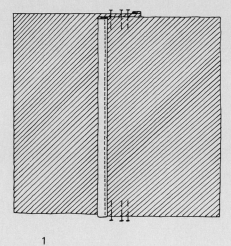

1

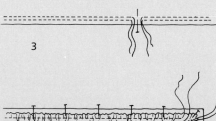

2

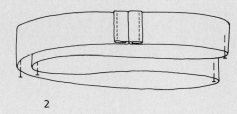

3

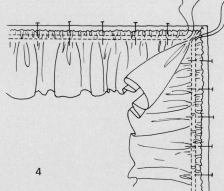

4

DIRECTIONS

1. Iron the fabric flat.

2. For the pillow front, cut a piece of fabric measuring 1 inch larger than the pillow form in both directions. (If you are using a patterned fabric, be sure to adjust it so that the design falls the way you like.)

3. For the pillow back, cut a piece of fabric measuring 1 inch larger than the form in one direction and 6 inches larger than the form in the other direction. Referring to Illustration 1, cut the back piece in half crosswise to make two back pieces. With the wrong side up, iron a ¼-inch fold along one long edge of one back piece. Turn the fold over itself, enclosing the raw edge, and iron. Stitch the fold down to make a rolled hem. Repeat for the second back piece. With the two back pieces wrong side up, overlap the hemmed edges so that the pillow back measures the same size as the pillow front. Pin the top and bottom edges to secure the overlap.

4. To prepare the ruffled trim, stitch a ¼-inch rolled hem (as described in Step 3) at each end of the ribbon or lace. With the right sides together, fold the ribbon or lace in half crosswise and stitch a ½-inch seam along the hemmed edges. Iron the seam open. Referring to Illustration 2, fold the ribbon or lace in half again and mark the fold of each quarter section with a pin. Unfold.

5. Starting at one of the pins on the ribbon or lace, machine-baste a row of stitches ⅜ inch away from the bottom edge, ending the stitching at the next pin and leaving some thread hanging at each end. Repeat between all the pins. In the same manner, baste a second row of stitching ¼ inch away from the bottom edge (Illustration 3). Remove the pins.

6. Gather each quarter of the ribbon or lace by pulling the basting threads until each section measures the length of one pillow side. Adjust the gathers so that they are even. With the right sides together, align the stitched edge of the ribbon or lace with the raw edge of the pillow front, pinning to secure; make sure there is a little extra fullness at the corners (Illustration 4). Baste the ribbon or lace to the pillow front along the ⅜-inch stitching line. Remove the pins.

7. With the right sides together, pin the pillow back to the pillow front, enclosing the ribbon or lace. Stitch a ½-inch seam all around. Remove the pins. Turn the pillow cover right side out through the back opening. Gently tug on the ruffle to pull the corners through. Iron.

8. Insert the pillow form through the back opening.

Preserving the Past

*new houses that evoke the
feeling of another time*

Although the houses in this chapter may appear to date from the 18th or 19th centuries, all were built within the last sixty years. It is a tribute to the homeowners that, through hours of meticulous research and careful attention to the smallest details, they have been able to create homes that preserve past traditions.

Each story is different. When one couple learned that the Greek Revival house they had been hoping to buy had burned to the ground, they decided to build a house that would capture the spirit of the old building that was lost. Another couple had always wanted an early Cape Cod cottage overlooking the water, but could not find one in the right location. The solution was to build their own classic Cape, planned to be exactly like an early cottage—right down to the door latches. The third homeowner bought a 1937 residence impeccably designed to replicate the mid-18th-century farmsteads of southeastern Pennsylvania, and has devoted a great deal of time to furnishing it with regional antiques that enhance its "historic" character.

The paneled doors on this Pennsylvania fireplace replicate a circa 1760 design.

Attention to Detail

The first time the present owner of this impressive residence just outside Philadelphia saw it, she knew immediately that it was the house she wanted to live in. By the time the home was offered on the market two years later, she had admired the rambling stone building on numerous occasions. "Until then, I had only viewed the house from the end of the driveway," she recalls, "but when I finally had the opportunity to step inside, it was more than I expected."

It was immediately apparent that great care

had been taken with the design of the house, which was commissioned in 1937 from the noted Philadelphia architect G. Edwin Brumbaugh. Brumbaugh was known particularly for his preservation work on hundreds of old buildings in Pennsylvania, including examples in the historic settlements of Valley Forge, Germantown, the Ephrata Cloister, and Washington Crossing Park. However, he was also responsible for many original designs that reflected his life-long interest in the architecture of the region.

For this particular house, Brumbaugh drew

A fine example of the Colonial Revival architecture that was particularly popular in the early decades of this century, the 1937 house at left was modeled after the 18th-century farmhouses of southeastern Pennsylvania. Fieldstone was used widely as a building material in the region; the door hood design is also indigenous to the area.

Continued

The carved mantelpiece and fireplace paneling in the living room, left, re-create 18th-century styles. The picture mounted on the overmantel shows a port scene; painted in Canton, China, in the 1800s, it was brought to Philadelphia as part of the China trade.

An elegant archway distinguishes the hall at right and frames an unusual 19th-century "waving-banner" Windsor settee, one of a pair. The large portrait hanging over the settee is a likeness of Catherine Dutton, a lifelong resident of Philadelphia; the small painting next to it depicts her granddaughter.

his ideas from the mid-18th-century farmhouses of southeastern Pennsylvania, although he did not copy any single residence. While he included many 20th-century improvements—such as structural steel—in the design, he also carefully replicated 18th-century features, based on his own research and on the measured drawings he made of early buildings.

Each built-in corner cupboard, for example, was made to scale from period pieces. The paneling on such cupboards and on the fireplace walls followed existing designs that date to around 1760. Moldings were planed to widths and patterns used by 18th-century craftsmen, and the chair rails were even positioned at precise heights. Brumbaugh believed strongly that

such meticulous attention to proportion and architectural detail was essential to evoking the overall feeling of another time, as well as to creating rooms where period furniture would fit in comfortably.

Although the structure was finished over half a century ago, this deep appreciation for the past was not lost on the current homeowner. In particular, she found that living in the house fostered her already healthy interest in American antiques. Family heirlooms, pieces carefully culled from antiques shops and shows, and even furnishings acquired from Brumbaugh's own estate now appear in every room.

In keeping with the regional character of the house, most of the furniture—which dates from

Continued

The corner cupboard in the dining room, above, is a copy of an 18th-century original from a house in Pottsgrove, Pennsylvania. Among the Chinese export porcelains on display are the punch bowl and pair of rare candlesticks on the Federal drop-leaf dining table.

The Federal-period tester bed above shows off a handsome quilt with an unusual, wide chintz border.

colonial times through the Federal period—was made in or near Philadelphia. The rose medallion and blue-and-white Canton export porcelains displayed in cupboards and on tabletops are also from that city, transported there by clipper ship during the 19th century at a time when local merchants were actively involved in America's China trade.

Finding early pieces of local significance, however, is only one aspect of the pleasure that the homeowner takes in period furnishings. Using antiques throughout the house also gives

her an opportunity to indulge an interest in textiles. Among her extensive collections can be found numerous samplers, needlework pictures, Oriental rugs, and 19th-century quilts; beautiful in themselves, such pieces also frequently serve to inspire the homeowner's choice of the fabrics she uses for curtains and bed hangings. Perhaps the primary appeal of antiques for this collector, however, is their versatility. "It's easy to decorate with antiques," she comments, "because the charming old pieces instantly bring warmth and comfort into a room."

A product of the China trade, the Cantonese-made desk in the bedroom above dates from around 1840.

139

TRADITIONAL SWAG CURTAIN

One of the prettiest and easiest ways to drape a window is with a swag curtain. Both the traditional swag at left, and the asymmetric version shown on the following pages, will suit most window sizes.

The traditional swag curtain is made by catching a length of fabric at the window corners with tiebacks so that the center falls into a curve. The width of the fabric determines the fullness of the curve, and you will need to measure and cut accordingly (see Step 3 in the Directions opposite).

A medium-weight fabric (one that drapes well, such as chintz) is recommended; if you are using a patterned fabric, avoid a design that is distinctly directional. A solid polished cotton was used here for the lining, which will show when the curtain sides, or legs, are gathered into shape.

MATERIALS

- Two curtain tiebacks
- Medium-weight fabric for curtain front (see Step 2 in Directions opposite for yardage)
- Medium-weight fabric for lining (same yardage as for swag)
- ⅛-inch cable cord (5 times width of fabric)
- 1 yard kitchen string
- Dressmakers' pins
- Seam ripper
- Small safety pin

DIRECTIONS

1. Install the tiebacks at the upper corners of the window following the manufacturer's directions.

2. To calculate the length of fabric required for both the curtain front and the lining, start by measuring the distance between the two tiebacks. Next, measure the distance from the shaft of one tieback down the side of the window to the place where you would like the curtain legs to end at their longest point; add 1 inch for seam allowance, then double this measurement. Add this figure to the measurement between the tiebacks.

3. Trim the selvages from both the curtain fabric and the lining fabric. Drape the curtain fabric loosely over the tiebacks and adjust the swag to the desired fullness. If the swag is too bulky, you will need to cut the fabric to a narrower width.

4. Remove the curtain fabric, and cut it narrower if necessary. Iron the fabric flat. Referring to Illustration 1, fold the fabric in half with the wrong sides together. Using a pencil, mark the fold on the right side of the fabric with the letter A; this mark will fall at the center of the swag. Measure out from point A half the distance between the two tiebacks and mark this point with the letter B on the right side of both layers of fabric.

5. Open the curtain fabric and, with the right side up, lay it flat. Cut the kitchen string into two equal lengths. Tie a piece of string around the fabric at each of the B marks. Drape the curtain fabric over the tiebacks, tying each string around a tieback. Adjust the swag to the desired fullness, making sure both legs of the swag are even.

6. Referring to Illustration 2, mark the letter C on the lower edge of the swag where each string now touches. Mark the letter D where you would like the inner corners of the legs to fall. Untie the strings and remove the curtain fabric from the tiebacks.

7. With the right side up, lay the curtain fabric flat. Measure to see if both points C are equidistant from point A and both points D are equidistant from their corresponding points C; if necessary, adjust the marks.

8. Referring to Illustration 3, fold the fabric in half with the wrong sides together so that points B, C, and D all correspond; lay flat. Draw a light pencil line between points B and C. With the fabric still folded, flip, and repeat on the other side. Mark a diagonal line from the top corner of the fabric down to point D. Cut along this line through both layers of fabric.

9. Using the curtain front as a pattern, cut out the lining fabric to match exactly. With the right sides together and the edges even, pin the curtain fabric to the lining fabric. Referring to Illustration 4, stitch a ½-inch seam around all four sides, leaving an 8-inch opening at the center of the top edge for turning. Remove the pins. Clip the corners, turn the swag right side out, and push out the corners using a scissors tip. Slipstitch the opening closed. Iron.

10. On the right side of the curtain, stitch through both layers of fabric along one of the pencil lines from points B to C. Stitch ⅜ inch away on each side of the first stitch line to form a double casing. Repeat for the other line from B to C. Using the seam ripper, open the ends of the casings.

11. Cut the cable cord into two equal lengths. Attach a small safety pin to one end of one piece of cord. Referring to Illustration 5, insert the pin into one side of one casing at point B. Work the pin and cord through the casing to point C, and up the other side back to point B. Remove the pin and leave the ends hanging loose. Repeat for the other casing.

12. Iron the curtain. Pull the cable cord ends to gather the swag. Drape the swag over the tiebacks and tie the cords to the tiebacks to anchor. Adjust the gathers and folds if necessary.

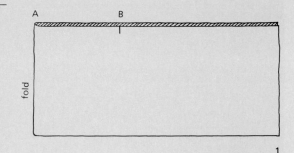

1

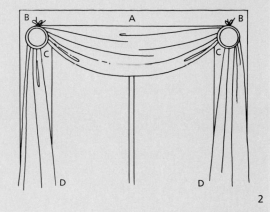

2

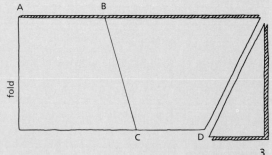

3

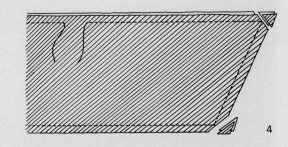

4

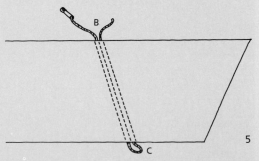

5

ASYMMETRIC
SWAG
CURTAIN

An asymmetric swag curtain is a good treatment for a corner window. Or a pair, pulled in opposing directions, can work well for two windows that are side by side. The curtain shown here is a simple rectangle, gathered at the top and drawn back into a gentle swag with a drawstring cord caught on a tieback. The shape of the swag depends on the distance of the tieback from the window bottom.

A medium-weight fabric (one that drapes well, such as chintz) is recommended; if you are using a patterned fabric, avoid a design that is distinctly horizontal. A solid polished cotton was used here for the lining, which will show when the swag is gathered back.

MATERIALS

- Dowel-type curtain rod
- Curtain tieback
- Medium-weight fabric for curtain front (see Step 3 in Directions opposite for yardage)
- Medium-weight fabric for lining (same yardage as for swag)
- ⅛-inch cable cord (4 times width of window)
- 2 yards decorative cording
- 1 yard kitchen string
- Measuring tape
- Dressmakers' pins
- Seam ripper
- Small safety pin

DIRECTIONS

1. Install the curtain rod according to the manufacturer's directions.

2. Determine the side of the window on which you want the tieback to be and install it at the desired height straight down from the rod bracket, following the manufacturer's directions.

3. To calculate the length of fabric required for both the curtain front and the lining, start by measuring the distance from the bottom of the curtain rod to the windowsill. Next, wrap the measuring tape loosely around the curtain rod and take this measurement for the rod casing. Add the two figures, then add an additional 6 inches. To calculate the width of the fabric required for the curtain front and the lining, measure the distance between the two rod brackets, multiply by 1½, and add 1 inch. If the final total is greater than the width your fabric comes in not counting the selvage (standard widths are 36, 48, 54, and 60 inches), you will need to buy an additional length of both the curtain front and the lining fabric.

4. Iron the fabric flat. Trim the selvages from both the curtain fabric and the lining fabric. If necessary, stitch two lengths of fabric together side by side to make curtain fabric and lining pieces that are large enough to cut to the dimensions calculated in Step 3. Cut out the curtain fabric. Cut out the lining fabric to the exact measurements of the curtain piece.

5. With the right sides together and the edges even, pin the curtain fabric to the lining fabric. Stitch a ½-inch seam around all four sides, leaving a 12-inch opening at the center of the top edge for turning. Remove the pins. Clip the corners, turn the swag right side out, and push out the corners using a scissors tip. Slipstitch the opening closed. Iron.

6. With the curtain lining facing up, measure down from the top edge 2½ inches, plus half the rod casing measurement, and mark a light pencil line from side to side; on this line, fold the top of the curtain over toward the lining, iron, and pin. Referring to Illustration 1, stitch through all thicknesses 2¼ inches down from the fold. Then stitch ¼ inch away from the finished edge to form the rod casing. Remove the pins.

7. Hang the curtain from the rod and gather the fabric into a swag by gently pulling it toward the tieback; using the kitchen string, tie the swag to the tieback. Adjust the string and the gathers so that the outside edge of the curtain falls straight along the frame of the window and the inside edge drapes gracefully. Referring to Illustration 2, use a pencil to mark the letter A at the place where the string touches the outside edge of the curtain; mark the letter B at the place where the string touches the inside edge of the curtain. Using pins, mark the fabric at a few points where it is touched by the string. Being careful not to disturb the pins, remove the string. Take the curtain down and lay it flat with the right side up.

8. With the pins as a guide, draw a light pencil line from point A to point B. Remove the pins. Stitch along the line through both layers of fabric. Stitch ⅜ inch away on each side of the first stitch line to form a double casing. Using the seam ripper, open both ends of the casing.

9. Attach a small safety pin to one end of the cable cord. Referring to Illustration 3, insert the safety pin into one side of the casing at point A. Work the pin and cord through the casing to point B, and up the other side back to point A. Remove the safety pin and leave the ends hanging loose.

10. Iron the curtain and hang it from the rod. Pull the cable cord ends to gather the swag. Tie the ends to the tieback to anchor; trim.

11. Wrap the decorative cording twice around the casing and tie to the tieback; trim if necessary.

A New Classic

Thus handsome red clapboard house represents a true labor of love for the Ohio couple who built it: over the course of several years, they kept their sleeves rolled up and lived amid ladders and sawdust while they did much of the work themselves. The effort devoted to this hands-on building project was worth it, however, as finishing the house meant realizing an idea that had been evolving for ten years before the foundation was ever laid.

Initially, that idea focused on a beautiful, yet derelict, 1820s Greek Revival homestead in their community. Each time the pair drove past the old house, they talked about buying and restoring it someday, but one Halloween night the building went up in flames. Virtually all that could be salvaged after the firemen left were the front door and the great stone doorstep, which the couple quickly arranged to buy. That done, there seemed only one obvious way to proceed: to build a new "old" house that would incorporate these distinctive architectural elements.

While they did not try to reproduce the old house exactly, the couple did choose a design that captures the spirit of the 1820s Greek Revival houses that proliferated in the Western Reserve area of Ohio. As was true of many early

Continued

Salvaged from an 1820s house, the classical front door on the residence at right is a hallmark of the Greek Revival style. Also typical are the corner pilasters and the symmetrical façade design.

Nineteenth-century folk potters in Pennsylvania and the Shenandoah Valley occasionally found time to make more than just utilitarian objects. Their glazed-redware figurines and toys, created as gifts for children and friends, now inspire contemporary pieces such as the hunter-and-bear design above.

dwellings erected by the eastern homesteaders who came to the region, the building resembles a New England farmhouse—but incorporates some of the distinguishing local Ohio characteristics that developed, such as the extra-wide exterior moldings and corner pilasters. The furnishings inside, in turn, reflect the heritage of another group that settled in the area: the Penn-

sylvania Germans. Assembled over the years, the collection comprises many Pennsylvania pieces, including painted chairs and chests, a *schrank*, or wardrobe, and several quilts and coverlets.

This multifaceted project began with the purchase of a wooded plot of land, where just enough trees were cleared to make space for the driveway and the house itself. (One owner's

Continued

Among the Pennsylvania-German pieces in the living room, above, are the two rockers, which date to the 1840s.

Attention to accurate architectural detail extended to the staircase moldings, opposite, which were copied from an early homestead in Ohio's Western Reserve. The bird tree on the chest recalls a Pennsylvania-German folk-art tradition; the birds were carved by friends of the homeowners.

The Ohio earthenware
fat lamp above was made
between 1835 and 1870. Oil
or grease was poured into
the center hole of the lamp
reservoir, and rag wicks
were placed in the spouts at
either side to draw the
oil up to the flame.

*Equipped with antique
utensils, an enormous
fireplace—often put to use
for cooking—dominates the
keeping room, left. The
bricks are a combination
of old, salvaged pieces
and new bricks chosen
to match.*

The cheerful breakfast room, right, features decorative contemporary redware pottery inspired by Pennsylvania-German styles.

enthusiasm for building in the old tradition was so great that he first tried cutting the trees down with an axe—but he quickly traded that tool in for a chain saw.) As soon as the shell of the house was completed and insulated, and the walls covered with plasterboard, the owners moved in, tackling almost all of the finishwork —painting, sanding, small carpentry projects, and even the installation of the heating system —by themselves. They also became expert at locating professionals skilled in traditional craftsmanship; among them was a mason who knew how to build a beehive oven, as well as a lumber company that was able to produce the sixteen-foot-long hand-hewn beams needed to span the length of their keeping room ceiling.

Continued

Shelves from an antique walnut pewter cupboard fit precisely on a breakfast room wall, above, creating additional display space. The ceramic pieces are examples of Routson pottery, which was made in the Ohio towns of Doylestown and Wooster in the 1800s.

Because the couple were not trying to create an exact replica of any particular dwelling, they felt free to incorporate whatever 19th-century features were of particular interest to them. In the rustic keeping room, for instance, they constructed a massive brick fireplace similar to those found in early, local farmhouses. A more sophisticated fireplace treatment, however, based on Pennsylvania-German wall paneling that they had admired at the Winterthur Museum, distinguishes the master bedroom. Antique architectural elements, including shelving and iron hardware bought at auctions, further enhance the period look of the house.

The fireplace wall in the master bedroom, above, was copied from an original that is now in the Winterthur Museum in Wilmington, Delaware. The grained decoration was carefully reproduced by a contemporary craftsman who also painted several pieces of furniture in the house.

A huge Pennsylvania-German schrank *dominates the bedroom at left. The 19th-century woven wool coverlet was also made in Pennsylvania.*

Hand-Carved Bird Trees

The fanciful painted wood sculptures known as bird trees are a folk tradition believed to have originated with the Pennsylvania Germans. Little is known about the history of the carvings, but one theory holds that such ornamental pieces were an outgrowth of egg trees—small trees that were decorated with carved or dyed eggs at Easter.

One of the few bird tree carvers known by name is "Schtochschnitzler," or "cane carver," Simmons, an itinerant craftsman who traveled through Berks and Lehigh counties in Pennsylvania in the late 1800s and early 1900s. The bird trees shown here include antique pieces by Simmons and other early carvers, as well as contemporary folk carvings.

This c. 1875 bird tree retains its original paint. One of a pair, it may have served as a mantel decoration.

Whimsical birds occupy the branches of this early Pennsylvania-German carving, done around 1820.

This contemporary piece was inspired by the bird trees created by early Pennsylvania-German carvers.

A bird tree carved by "Schtochschnitzler" Simmons suggested the design for this contemporary piece.

Sassafras branches dried to shape were used to make these new trees; the birds were carved with a penknife.

"Schtochschnitzler" Simmons carved this yellow pine bird tree around the turn of the century.

An itinerant black folk artist carved this c. 1920 tree, one of two he created for his wife and daughter.

The contemporary artist who made these pieces originated his own blackbird and partridge designs.

A Country Cape

Details such as the traditional black-and-white coloring of the chimney and the row of small windows, or "lights," over the front door make the recently built Cape Cod cottage above almost indistinguishable from its colonial-era counterparts.

After years of traveling from Pennsylvania to Cape Cod, Massachusetts, for summer vacations, the couple that own this seaside house decided to make the Cape their permanent home. They had always loved the small 18th- and 19th-century shingled cottages associated with the region, but most of the old buildings that they found for sale were situated on back roads, far removed from any water views. For this family, the solution was to purchase an acre of land overlooking a cove, and to build their own "early" Cape Cod cottage.

Now, less than a decade after the house was completed, the cedar shingles are weathered to a silvery gray, and vines climb over the front doorway, making it virtually impossible to tell that the residence has not been on this site for the last two hundred years. Indeed, with its characteristic pitched roof stopping just above the front windows and door, the cottage displays a classic one-and-one-half-story Cape Cod design. In order to ensure a convincing look, the owners were particularly attentive to scale; from roof pitch to window dimensions and chimney size, the house's proportions were carefully worked out according to those found in the designs of its historic counterparts.

Throughout, the owners worked closely with a local builder, who shared their enthusiasm for the project. This seasoned professional was not

Continued

A small, central stair hall like that at left is a typical feature of Cape Cod cottages. The iron latch on the door was handwrought by a local craftsman, as was all of the hardware in the house.

Part of the keeping room, left, is used as an informal living room. The long fireplace mantel was salvaged from an early house, while the new closet door below it was made to look old.

Country French pieces furnish an informal dining area, above, at one end of the keeping room.

only able to successfully incorporate salvaged architectural elements, such as mantelpieces, that the couple planned to use in their new house, but was also instrumental in locating a source for compatible materials. Among these are the wide pine floorboards, which, laid in random widths, add significantly to the 18th-century look of the rooms.

Another professional, a carpenter who specializes in fine woodwork and "antique" finishes, made all of the paneling and moldings in the house, and "distressed" the surfaces of the

floors and wood cabinets to give them a time-worn appearance. Moreover, no detail was overlooked; even the door latches, hinges, and other iron hardware in the house were handmade by craftsmen on Cape Cod.

True to tradition, the layout of the rooms follows the basic center-chimney floor plan of a typical Cape Cod cottage, in which two rooms, opening off a central stair hall on the first floor, are situated at the front of the house. As it would have been in the past, one of these rooms, the parlor, is finished as the "best" room, with paint-

Continued

The paneling and plastered ceiling in the parlor, above, distinguish it as the "best" room in the house.

Serving as pantry storage, wooden boxes like those above were used in most American households through the 19th century. Old boxes found today usually date from the 1800s; original paint increases their value.

ed paneling, a plastered ceiling, and enclosed ceiling beams. By contrast, the large keeping room, which extends across the rear of the house, is far more rustic in character, with exposed beams, plain plaster walls, and a rough wood-plank ceiling. Boasting an impressive fireplace, this room is the heart of the home, used as a casual living and dining area.

The one nod to modern times, perhaps, is the up-to-date kitchen, located in a small, one-story wing. On the exterior, the kitchen wing was designed to suggest the little additions that typically jut from the sides of early Cape Cod cottages. On the inside, however, a cathedral ceiling and skylights give the room an open, spacious feeling. While the kitchen is efficient and practical, it also has a warm, country look. The cabinets were custom-made with paneled

Continued

Above, vintage decorated stoneware pitchers from France are mixed with a collection of pewter—mostly 19th-century pieces from Pennsylvania—for a striking kitchen display. The painted wooden firkins, or buckets, on top of the hutch are American.

*Situated unobtrusively
between hand-hewn beams,
skylights admit plenty of
sunshine into the cheery
kitchen, left.*

163

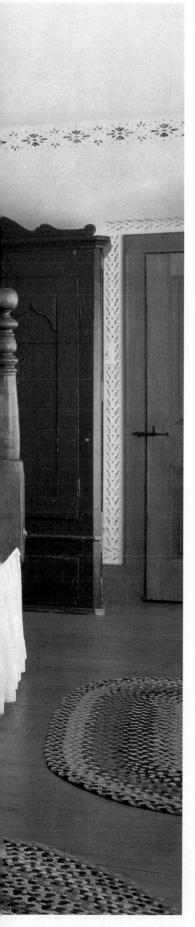

doors and wooden pulls, and were painted an "old" red color to suggest the finish of antique dry sinks and cupboards. The wood floors and the hand-hewn beams in the ceiling were also carefully designed to blend with those in the keeping room.

The same sense of tradition extends to the master bedroom, where the stenciled wall borders, based on colonial designs, recall an era when such decorative painting was the country dweller's practical substitute for expensive wallpapers. But the room does not exist entirely in the past; there is plenty of built-in closet space, for example, which would have been absent in an 18th-century Cape Cod cottage. In fact, for these homeowners, it is conveniences such as this that make a "reproduction" house a great alternative to the real thing.

A blue-and-white color scheme creates a light, summery effect in the master bedroom. Here, new and old are mixed effectively: the pieced quilt on the bed, left, was made recently in an Amish community, while the ornate wicker chair and lace tablecloth in the sitting area, above, are antiques.

Decor for the Door

The tradition of mounting an iron or brass knocker on a front door harks back to a time before electric bells or buzzers were at hand to alert the inhabitants of a house that someone had come calling. Aside from its usefulness, the knocker also provided a decorative touch—an extravagance, perhaps, that a thrifty homeowner would have considered with care.

The first door knockers to be made in America were of iron. Beginning in the early 18th century, they could be purchased from the local blacksmith, even in the smallest villages. Cast-brass knockers were also available from the time of the early colonies, but most were imported from England and were considerably more expensive than those made of iron.

While forged knockers generally took simple forms, such as bell or strap shapes, cast knockers were often more elaborate and might reflect the taste of the times. Eagle- and shield-shaped knockers, for example, were especially popular during the Federal period, when classical motifs were in vogue. Aside from fashion, the shape of a door knocker might also convey a message: a nautical or animal motif could suggest a homeowner's hobby, while a pineapple—the traditional symbol of welcome—offered a friendly greeting.

Today a traditional wrought-iron or brass knocker on the front door adds greatly to the period feeling of a house. Reproduction knockers like those at right are widely available from specialty hardware companies.

Selected Reading

Birren, Faber. *Creative Color*. West Chester, Pa.: Schiffer Publishing, 1987.

Bishop, Adele, and Cile Lord. *The Art of Decorative Stenciling*. New York: Penguin Books, 1976.

Boyce, Charles. *Dictionary of Furniture*. New York: Facts on File Publications, 1985.

Brittain, Judy, ed. *Terence Conran's Home Furnishings*. Boston: Little, Brown & Company, 1986.

Busch, Akiko. *Floorworks: Bringing Rooms to Life with Surface Design and Decoration*. Toronto: Bantam Books, 1988.

Comstock, Helen, ed. *The Concise Encyclopedia of American Antiques*. New York: Hawthorn Books, n.d.

Conran, Terence. *The House Book*. New York: Crown Publishers, 1982.

Cooke, Edward S., Jr., ed. *Upholstery in America from the Seventeenth Century to World War I*. New York: W.W. Norton & Company, 1987.

Dittrick, Mark, and Diane Kender Dittrick. *Decorative Hardware*. New York: Hearst Books, 1982.

Eastwood, Maud. *Antique Builders' Hardware: Knobs and Accessories*. Beaverton, Oreg.: Lithtex Printing, 1982.

Fernandez, Genevieve. *American Traditional: A Comprehensive Guide to Home Decorating the Ethan Allen Way*. New York: Simon and Schuster, 1984.

Fleming, John, Hugh Honour, and Nikolaus Pevsner. *The Penguin Dictionary of Architecture*. New York: Penguin Books, 1966.

Gilliatt, Mary. *Decorating: A Realistic Guide*. New York: Pantheon Books, 1977.

Gilliatt, Mary. *The Complete Book of Home Design*. Boston: Little, Brown & Company, 1984.

Gray, Linda, with Jocasta Innes. *The Complete Book of Decorating Techniques*. Boston: Little, Brown & Company, 1986.

Grow, Lawrence. *Architectural Painting*. New York: Rizzoli, 1986.

Hague, William E., ed. *The Complete Basic Book of Home Decorating*. Garden City, N.Y.: Doubleday & Company, 1968.

Harris, Cyril M., ed. *Illustrated Dictionary of Historic Architecture*. New York: Dover Publications, 1977.

Hornung, Clarence P. *Treasury of American Design: A Pictorial Survey of Popular Folk Arts*. New York: Harry N. Abrams, 1971.

Innes, Jocasta. *Paint Magic*. New York: Pantheon Books, 1981.

Irwin, John Rice. *Baskets and Basket Makers in Southern Appalachia*. Exton, Pa.: Schiffer Publishing, Ltd., 1982.

Kauffman, Henry J. *The American Farmhouse*. New York: Bonanza Books, 1988.

Kendrick, A.F., and C.E.C. Tattersall. *Hand-Woven Carpets: Oriental and European*. New York: Dover Publications, 1973.

Kopp, Joel, and Kate Kopp. *American Hooked and Sewn Rugs: Folk Art Underfoot*. New York: E.P. Dutton, 1985.

Le Grice, Lyn. *The Art of Stencilling*. New York: Clarkson N. Potter, 1986.

Lipman, Jean, and Tom Armstrong, eds. *American Folk Painters of Three Centuries*. New York: Hudson Hills Press, 1980.

Lipman, Jean, and Alice Winchester. *The Flowering of American Folk Art, 1776-1876*. New York: Viking Press, 1974.

Lott, Jane. *The Conran Home Decorator: Floors and Flooring*. New York: Villard Books, 1986.

Lynn, Catherine. *Wallpaper in America from the Seventeenth Century to World War I*. New York: W.W. Norton & Company, 1980.

Mayhew, Edgar deN., and Minor Myers, Jr. *A Documentary History of American Interiors from the Colonial Era to 1915*. New York: Charles Scribner's Sons, 1980.

Miller, Judith, and Martin Miller. *Period Details: A Sourcebook for House Restoration*. New York: Crown Publishers, 1987.

Montgomery, Florence M. *Textiles in America, 1650-1870*. New York: W.W. Norton & Company, 1984.

Niesewand, Nonie. *The Home Style Book*. New York: Whitney Library of Design, 1984.

Nylander, Richard C. *Wallpapers for Historic Buildings: A Guide to Selecting Reproduction Wallpapers*. Washington, D C.: Preservation Press, 1983.

Nylander, Richard C., Elizabeth Redmond, and Penny J. Sander. *Wallpaper in New England*. Boston: Society for the Preservation of New England Antiquities, 1986.

O'Neil, Isabel. *The Art of the Painted Finish for Furniture and Decoration*. New York: William Morrow & Company, 1971.

Pettit, Florence H. *America's Printed and Painted Fabrics 1600-1900*. New York: Hastings House, 1970.

Rorabaugh, W.J. *The Alcoholic Republic, An American Tradition*. New York: Oxford University Press, 1981.

Pile, John F. *Interior Design*. New York: Harry N. Abrams, 1988.

Rice, Kym S. *Early American Taverns: For the Entertainment of Friends and Strangers*. Chicago: Regnery Gateway, 1983.

Schiffer, Herbert, Peter Schiffer, and Nancy Schiffer. *Antique Iron: Survey of American and English Forms, Fifteenth through Nineteenth Centuries*. Exton, Pa.: Schiffer Publishing, 1979.

Seale, William. *Recreating the Historic House Interior*. Nashville: American Association for State and Local History, 1979.

Slayton, Mariette Paine. *Early American Decorating Techniques: Step-by-Step Directions for Mastering Traditional Crafts*. New York: Macmillan Company, 1972.

Smith, Carter. *Decorating with Americana: How to Know It, Where to Find It, and How to Make It Work for You*. Birmingham, Ala.: Oxmoor House, 1985.

Stephenson, Sue H. *Basketry of the Appalachian Mountains*. New York: Prentice Hall Press, 1986.

Sudjic, Deyan, ed. *The House Style Book*. New York: Holt, Rinehart & Winston, 1984.

Waring, Janet. *Early American Stencils on Walls and Furniture*. New York: Dover Publications, 1968.

Weissman, Judith Reiter, and Wendy Lavitt. *Labors of Love: America's Textiles and Needlework, 1650-1930*. New York: Alfred A. Knopf, 1987.

Wetherbee, Jean. *A Second Look at White Ironstone*. Lombard, Ill.: Wallace-Homestead Book Company, 1985.

Wilson, José, and Arthur Leaman. *Decorating American Style*. Boston: New York Graphic Society, 1975.

Wilson, Kax. *A History of Textiles*. Boulder, Colo.: Westview Press, 1979.

Woodard, Thos. K., and Blanche Greenstein. *Twentieth Century Quilts, 1910-1950*. New York: E.P. Dutton, 1988.

Photography and Illustration Credits

Cover, frontispiece, and pages 10-21, 29 (right), 34-47, 78-85 (except 83 right), 130, 132-139, 144-153, 156-165 (except 162 left): George Ross. Pages 8, 26-31 (except 29 right): Dennis Krukowski. Pages 22, 23, 24, 25, 32-33, 48-49, 52-57, 60, 62-67, 70-75, 86-87, 88, 98-99, 100-107, 110, 112-119, 120-121, 122-127, 128, 140, 142, 166-167: Steven Mays. Pages 50-51: George W. Gardner. Pages 58-59: courtesy of the American Antiquarian Society, Worcester, MA. Page 68: (both) courtesy of the DeWitt Historical Society of Tompkins County, Ithaca, NY. Page 69: (clockwise from top left) Western History Collections, University of Oklahoma Library, Norman, OK; courtesy of the DeWitt Historical Society of Tompkins County, Ithaca, NY; Culver Pictures, Inc.; Solomon D. Butcher Collection, Nebraska State Historical Society, Lincoln, NE; Colorado His-

torical Society, Denver, CO. Pages 76-77: (top row, left to right) Grant Heilman Photography, Inc./Grant Heilman; Grant Heilman Photography, Inc./Larry Lefever; f/Stop Pictures, Inc./Laurance B. Aiuppy; Grant Heilman Photography, Inc./Larry Lefever; (second row, left to right) f/Stop Pictures, Inc./Alan L. Graham; Grant Heilman Photography, Inc./Larry Lefever; Grant Heilman Photography, Inc./Larry Lefever; Grant Heilman Photography, Inc./Larry Lefever; (third row, left to right) Seitz and Seitz, Inc./Blair Seitz; f/Stop Pictures, Inc./Thomas Ames, Jr.; f/Stop Pictures, Inc./Laurance B. Aiuppy; Grant Heilman Photography, Inc./John Colwell; (bottom row, left to right) Grant Heilman Photography, Inc./Grant Heilman; f/Stop Pictures, Inc./Clyde H. Smith; Grant Heilman Photography, Inc./Grant Heilman; f/Stop Pictures, Inc./Clyde H. Smith. Page 83: (right)

Schecter Lee. Pages 90-97: Rick Patrick. Page 108: portrait used with special permission from Berea College and the Doris Ulmann Foundation, Berea, KY. Pages 108-109: basket photographs © 1990 Cynthia W. Taylor and Rachel Nash Law, from their forthcoming book "Appalachian White Oak Basketmaking: Handing Down the Basket," The University of Tennessee Press, Knoxville, TN, 1990. Pages 154-155: (top row, left to right) collection of the Museum of American Folk Art, NYC, gift of Mr. and Mrs. Arthur Fine; Steven Mays; Steven Mays; courtesy of The Henry Francis du Pont Winterthur Museum, Winterthur, DE; (bottom row, left to right) Steven Mays; Philadelphia Museum of Art, Philadelphia, PA, John D. McIlhenny Collection; Steven Mays; Steven Mays; Steven Mays; Steven Mays. Page 162: (left) Jon Elliott. Pages 129, 141, 143: illustrations by Ray Skibinski.

Prop Credits

The Editors would like to thank the following for their contributions as designers or consultants or for their courtesy in lending items for photography. Items not listed below are privately owned. **Cover**: wall stenciling—Nona Gehman, Leola, PA; 18th-century restoration carpentry and millwork—Gene Shaw, The Wooden Plane, Lancaster, PA. **Page 8**: interior designed and decorated by Tonin MacCallum, NYC. **Pages 10-21**: wall stenciling and grain-painting on doors—Nona Gehman, Leola, PA; floor stenciling—Kenneth T. Fortney, Columbia, PA; 18th-century restoration carpentry and millwork—Gene Shaw, The Wooden Plane, Lancaster, PA. **Pages 22-23**: sponge-painting on wall—Dan Sevigny, Brooklyn, NY. **Pages 24-25**: sponging samples—Dan Sevigny, Brooklyn, NY. **Pages 26-31**: interiors designed and decorated by Tonin MacCallum, NYC. **Pages 32-33**: antique quilts courtesy of

Thos. K. Woodard, American Antiques & Quilts; antique wicker furniture—The Wicker Garden, NYC; cotton rug—ABC Carpet and Home, NYC. **Pages 34-47**: photographed at "Quaker Hill," the restored home of Richard and Sue Studebaker. **Pages 48-49**: antique ironstone from the collection of Thomas and Olga Moreland, NY. **Pages 50-57**: interiors designed by Nelson Ferlita. **Page 53**: small floral paintings above couch—Ed Dier, El Macero, CA. **Pages 54-55**: pottery—Ron Dier, Hillsdale, NY. **Page 56**: floral paintings—Ed Dier, El Macero, CA. **Pages 60-67**: architectural design—Phillip Kelley Architectural Design, Zionsville, PA. **Pages 70-75**: architectural design—Mark Zeff Design, Inc., NYC. **Pages 80-85**: interiors by C. F. Brasch and J. H. Kistler/The Barn at Fry's Run, Easton, PA. **Pages 86-87**: antique glass bottles—Joe Stamp/Funchie, Bunkers, Gaks, and Gleeks, NYC. **Pages**

98-99: Log Cabin quilt and log cabin collection—James Cramer and Dean Johnson, Keedysville, MD. **Pages 108-109**: consultants—Cynthia W. Taylor, Marietta, OH, and Rachel Nash Law, Fayetteville, WV; all baskets (except top left and middle left) from the collection of Cynthia W. and Michael B. Taylor; (top left) from the collection of Rachel Nash Law and H. Wayne Law; (middle left) from the collection of Bruce Rigsby. **Pages 112-119**: antiques—Pantry & Hearth, NYC. **Pages 120-121**: all tiles courtesy of and available from Country Floors, NYC. **Page 146**: redware hunter-and-bear figurine in margin—Foltz Pottery, Reinholds, PA; folk-art birds on bird tree—Dan Strawser, Thompson Station, TN, Walter Gottshall, Reinholds, PA, and John Carlton, Sharptown, MD; whale and tramp-art eagle wall box—Walter Gottshall; grain-painting on candlebox and blanket chest—Sharon Sexton, Worthington,

OH; Lehnware (turned wooden cups)—June Gottshall, Reinholds, PA. **Page 147**: contemporary redware pottery—Breininger Pottery, Robesonia, PA, and Foltz Pottery, Reinholds, PA. **Pages 150-151**: comb-back Windsor chairs—Richard Grell, The Windsor Chairmaker, Hudson, OH; contemporary redware pottery—Breininger Pottery, Robesonia, PA, and Foltz Pottery, Reinholds, PA; folk-art bird tree—Dan Strawser, Thompson Station, TN. **Pages 152-153**: grain-painting on mantel and blanket chest—Sharon Sexton, Worthington, OH; Lancaster County Amish crib quilts—A Country Tradition, Wooster, OH; folk-art stork, pig, and bird on left in window—Walter Gottshall, Reinholds, PA; folk-art rocking goat and bird on right in windows—Dan Strawser, Thompson Station, TN; miniature stoneware—Caroline Curren, Glens Falls, NY. **Page 154**: bird trees: (bottom left) carved by John Carlton, Quantico, MD; (bottom right) carved by Walter Gottshall, Reinholds, PA. **Page 155**: bird trees: (top left) carved by Dan Strawser, Thompson Station, TN; (bottom left) from the collection of Frank Gaglio and Kathleen Molnar-Gaglio, Wurtzboro, NY; (bottom center and right) carved by John Carlton, Quantico, MD. **Pages 156-165**: interiors designed by Lucille Danneman, Orleans, MA. **Pages 166-167**: door knockers: (top row, left to right) "horse's head," brass, #12060—Restoration Works, Inc., Buffalo, NY; "dome shield," brass, #3107—Historic Housefitters Co., Brewster, NY; "pineapple," forged iron, #37—Williamsburg Blacksmiths, Williamsburg, MA; "perched eagle," brass, #3111—Historic Housefitters Co.; "#35," forged iron—Williamsburg Blacksmiths; "plain shield," brass, #3104—Historic Housefitters Co.; (middle row, left to right) "small lion," brass, #07667—Restoration Works, Inc.; "S-curl," forged iron, #40—Williamsburg Blacksmiths; "pineapple," brass, #3022—Historic Housefitters Co.; "eagle," brass, #07467—Restoration Works, Inc.; "anchor and rope," brass, #08067—Restoration Works, Inc.; "colonial," iron, #1904-1—Historic Housefitters Co.; "large eagle," brass, #3110—Historic Housefitters Co.; "#31," forged iron—Williamsburg Blacksmiths; (bottom row, left to right) "bell," brass, #3119—Historic Housefitters Co.; "#39," forged iron—Williamsburg Blacksmiths; "long rope," brass, #07369—Restoration Works, Inc.; "large lion," brass, #69—Restoration Works, Inc.; "fox," brass, #10669—Restoration Works, Inc.; "loop," brass, #3114—Historic Housefitters Co.

Index

Acknowledgments

Our thanks to Richard Anders, Susan and Richard Berman, C. F. Brasch, Lucille and Robert Danneman, Kay and George Davis, Ron Dier, Lani Groves, Earl Jameson, Judith A. Jedlicka, Phillip Kelley, Gloria and Frank Kennedy, Donald E. LeFever, Gail Lettick, John Lewis of the Berea College Museum, Paul and Anne Locher, Steve Love, Tonin MacCallum, Renae A. Mendall, Susan Peery, Janet Russo, Sue and Richard Studebaker, Jean Weatherbee, and Mark Zeff.

First printing
Published simultaneously in Canada
School and library distribution by Silver Burdett Company, Morristown, New Jersey

TIME-LIFE is a trademark of Time Incorporated U.S.A.

Production by Giga Communications, Inc.
Printed in U.S.A.

Library of Congress Cataloging-in-Publication Data

A Country house tour
p.   cm. — (American country)
ISBN 0-8094-6837-9 — ISBN 0-8094-6838-7 (lib. bdg.)
1. Interior decoration—United States.
2. Decoration and ornament, Rustic—United States.
3. Antiques in interior decoration.
I. Time-Life Books.   II. Series.
NK2002.C595   1990   747.213—dc20   90-31950
CIP

American Country was created by Rebus, Inc., and published by Time-Life Books.

REBUS, INC.

Publisher: RODNEY FRIEDMAN • Editor: MARYA DALRYMPLE
Executive Editor: RACHEL D. CARLEY • Managing Editor: BRENDA SAVARD • Consulting Editor: CHARLES L. MEE, JR.
Senior Editor: SUSAN B. GOODMAN • Copy Editor: ALEXA RIPLEY BARRE
Writers: JUDITH CRESSY, ROSEMARY G. RENNICKE • Freelance Writer: JOE L. ROSSON
Design Editors: NANCY MERNIT, CATHRYN SCHWING
Test Kitchen Director: GRACE YOUNG • Editor, The Country Letter: BONNIE J. SLOTNICK
Editorial Assistant: LEE CUTRONE • Contributing Editors: ANNE MOFFAT, DEE SHAPIRO
Indexer: MARILYN FLAIG

Art Director: JUDITH HENRY • Associate Art Director: SARA REYNOLDS
Designers: AMY BERNIKER, TIMOTHY JEFFS
Photographer: STEVEN MAYS • Photo Editor: SUE ISRAEL
Photo Assistant: ROB WHITCOMB • Freelance Photographer: GEORGE ROSS
Freelance Photo Stylist: VALORIE FISHER

Series Consultants: BOB CAHN, HELAINE W. FENDELMAN, LINDA C. FRANKLIN, GLORIA GALE,
KATHLEEN EAGEN JOHNSON, JUNE SPRIGG, CLAIRE WHITCOMB

Time-Life Books Inc. is a wholly owned subsidiary of THE TIME INC. BOOK COMPANY.

President and Chief Executive Officer: KELSO F. SUTTON
President, Time Inc. Books Direct: CHRISTOPHER T. LINEN

TIME-LIFE BOOKS INC.

Editor: GEORGE CONSTABLE
Director of Design: LOUIS KLEIN • Director of Editorial Resources: PHYLLIS K. WISE
Director of Photography and Research: JOHN CONRAD WEISER

President: JOHN M. FAHEY JR.
Senior Vice Presidents: ROBERT M. DeSENA, PAUL R. STEWART, CURTIS G. VIEBRANZ, JOSEPH J. WARD
Vice Presidents: STEPHEN L. BAIR, BONITA L. BOEZEMAN, MARY P. DONOHOE, STEPHEN L. GOLDSTEIN,
JUANITA T. JAMES, ANDREW P. KAPLAN, TREVOR LUNN, SUSAN J. MARUYAMA, ROBERT H. SMITH
New Product Development: TREVOR LUNN, DONIA ANN STEELE
Supervisor of Quality Control: JAMES KING

Publisher: JOSEPH J. WARD

For information about any Time-Life book please call 1-800-621-7026, or write:
Reader Information, Time-Life Customer Service
P.O. Box C-32068, Richmond, Virginia 23261-2068

Time-Life Books Inc. offers a wide range of fine recordings, including a Rock 'n' Roll Era series.
For subscription information, call 1-800-621-7026, or write TIME-LIFE MUSIC,
P.O. Box C-32068, Richmond, Virginia 23261-2068.